On Becoming a Teacher

On Becoming a Teacher

Edmund M. Kearney
Department of Psychology, Lewis University, Romeoville, IL, USA

SENSE PUBLISHERS
ROTTERDAM/BOSTON/TAIPEI

A C.I.P. record for this book is available from the Library of Congress.

ISBN: 978-94-6209-390-4 (paperback)
ISBN: 978-94-6209-391-1 (hardback)
ISBN: 978-94-6209-392-8 (e-book)

Published by: Sense Publishers,
P.O. Box 21858,
3001 AW Rotterdam,
The Netherlands
https://www.sensepublishers.com/

Printed on acid-free paper

This book is dedicated to the many master teachers I have had the good fortune of studying. I am sure there were many more I have inadvertently left off of the list, but these few deserve special mention:

Jeanne Day
Kathleen Disselhorst
Sr. Florence Marie Gerdes
Stanley Hauerwas
Katherine Helm
Edmund W. Kearney
Mary Jane Kearney
Eugene Kennedy
Ray Kizelevicus
Fr. Mark Link
Leslie Martin
Mark McDaniel
P.J. O'Mara
Mike Pressley
Jill Reich
Alan Rosenwald
Michael Schulein
Roger Wiers
John Zeunik

"My dear, haven't you realized that it is <u>you</u> they are studying most?"
Mary Jane Kearney's mentor, and then
Mary Jane Kearney to every educator she mentored.

"It is your privilege to be employed in teaching."
St. John Baptiste de La Salle

TABLE OF CONTENTS

Part V Teaching

Part VI Improving Your Craft

Part VII Conclusions

ACKNOWLEDGEMENTS

This book would not have been possible without the support and suggestions of my wife, Cristine. Thanks for doing more than just tolerating my "figaries."

A special thanks to Dr. Jeanette Mines, Academic Associate to the Provost and former Dean, College of Education, Lewis University for her review and comments on an earlier draft of this manuscript.

Thanks to Nancy Hanley and Christine Morrow for their optimistic attitude and clerical support of this project.

Sincere thanks to Robert Kearney for his advice, support, and suggestions regarding this project. We all aspire to write as well as you.

INTRODUCTION

This book is intended for all who love teaching and for all of us who aspire to be great teachers. Learning to teach is a lifelong journey that is exhilarating and frustrating, demanding and rewarding, and certainly unending. It is my hope that the thoughts and ideas shared in this book can contribute a small piece to the process of you becoming an excellent teacher.

Although this book is addressed directly to new teachers and those just learning the craft, I am hopeful that there are lessons within for teachers at all levels of experience and expertise. While I obviously believe that those learning to teach should seriously reflect on the twenty-five topics raised herein, I found it helpful to reconsider these same issues as I wrote. Even if you are an experienced teacher, reading these essays might affect you similarly, possibly even rekindling in you some dormant passions that have lost some of their power along the way.

Being a teacher is truly a societal privilege. It is not for everyone and comes with great responsibilities and demands. You are molding lives. You must, therefore, make a commitment to the lifelong process of learning in general, and to the specific task of mastering the craft of teaching. To do less than this is to squander the opportunity and perhaps even abuse the privilege.

This book is not an instructional manual. While a great many topics are covered, many are not. Certainly the reader will not find all of his or her answers here. Rather, I am hopeful that the reader discovers an opportunity to think deeply about essential components of both teaching and learning.

This book is written as a collection of brief essays, each followed by a few questions for either reflection or discussion. It is divided into six content sections, bookended by an introductory and conclusory essay. In Part I, I introduce you to the journey that awaits you. In Part II, I address the essential attributes of a great teacher. Part III is devoted to creating a positive and empowering classroom culture. Part IV explores the importance of knowing your students from multiple perspectives. Part V directly addresses teaching in the classroom. Finally, Part VI focuses on becoming better at your work throughout your career.

In the end, this book is intended for all of us who love teaching. In writing it, I am hopeful that I can include you in my community of learners as we explore this exciting process together. As such, I welcome your thoughts as you read, at the end, or later in your journey. Please do not hesitate to share them with me and thank you for letting me lead a part of your journey if only for this brief time.

Edmund M. Kearney
kearneed@lewisu.edu

PART I

BEGINNING THE JOURNEY

In this section you will be invited to begin the exciting journey into the world of education and teaching. This journey began with your choice to become a teacher, but is rooted in all of your life experiences.

CHOOSING WISELY: YOUR JOURNEY BEGINS WITH A SINGLE CHOICE

KEY TAKEAWAY

You have chosen a wonderful and challenging profession. You have made an exciting choice that will keep you engaged and stimulated throughout your lifetime. You will help many students and influence many lives. Enjoy the journey!

Congratulations on your decision to become a teacher. Whether you are just starting out, or perhaps have been at this for years, you should be praised for your decision to commit your life to the betterment of our great society.

While you might not be fully aware of it, in this one choice you have really made several life-altering decisions. Whether you have chosen to help elementary school children build a strong foundation, guide middle school students through turbulent years, prepare high school students for higher education, or help college students master their discipline, you will have an incredible impact on their lives. And in making this decision, you have chosen an incredible life journey for yourself as well.

You have chosen to defy the crowd. You have heard the litany of negative comments: "American schools are broken"; "Kids these days can't learn"; "Parents constantly interfere"; "Teachers are overpaid." You understand the ridiculousness of these broad statements. You likely believe that the United States can still provide the incredible education that makes us world leaders, that kids these days are no different than kids have always been, that parents simply want the best for their children, and that we all deserve to be compensated appropriately for the hard work we take on. Good for you.

It is easy to criticize from the sidelines. It is easy to judge harshly, to draw quick conclusions, to jump on bandwagons. But you have chosen to do none of these things. You have instead chosen to become part of the solution, rather than simply add to the problem of negativity. You have chosen the better path, the higher road. You have chosen the positive, the optimistic, and the hopeful path over the cynical and dismissive one. Good for you.

You have chosen to build rather than destroy, to contribute rather than to tax. It takes very little energy to tear down. It takes little skill to swing the wrecking ball willy-nilly with little or no concern for collateral damage. You must be a craftsman though to build skillfully. You must plan while being agile, adept, creative, persevering, and careful. You have chosen these as the attributes you value. Good for you.

You have chosen to embrace a challenge. Of course every day will not be easy. In fact, many days will be trying and challenging. Would you really want it any other way? To succeed in the face of adversity, to persevere when others retreat, to stay the course when others relinquish, these bring the joy and excitement to life. You have chosen to win the difficult battle. Good for you.

You have chosen to connect rather than to disengage. Connection takes energy and is risky. Connecting requires action, sometimes with bold strokes. Disengagement is passive. You know that others might not reciprocate. But you don't worry about that. That would be too risk averse, too cautious for someone who believes that people will be fundamentally better because of those connections. So you reach out. Good for you.

You have chosen to focus on potential rather than limitations. You know that we all can learn, even if many of us do so differently than the majority. You know that we all have so much to offer if that potential can be validated and tapped. Again it is easy to focus on what others cannot do. The list for all of us is endless. We may only be good at a few things, but we are all mediocre at many. So what. You have chosen to help others find those few good things. Good for you.

You have chosen to be a professional. In so doing you have accepted the fact that you have made a pact with society. You will follow certain rules and be held to a high standard. You will have certain responsibilities and privileges. You will accept feedback and criticism, and grow through the process. You will understand that you are one piece in a much larger, highly complex system. But even in accepting this, you will stay committed to your belief that one person can make a real difference. Good for you.

In essence, you have chosen a life of helping others. And here is a treat. Along the way you will have great fun. You will meet interesting people, engage in stimulating conversation, think deeply, connect, cope with frustration and failure, and celebrate many successes. You will grow as a human being. You will laugh a lot, cry some, and cling to hope. And all the while you will continue to learn. What a life you will lead all because of this one decision. Enjoy the journey.

Questions for Reflection and Discussion

1. You have chosen to become a teacher. Does this choice that you have made scare you or excite you? What about it is scary? What about it is exciting?
2. How did you come to this choice? What life factors have led you to this decision point?
3. Was this a hard or easy decision? What is your understanding of why this was hard or easy for you to make this decision?

UNDERSTANDING WHERE YOU CAME FROM: APPRECIATING YOUR APPRENTICESHIP

KEY TAKEAWAY

Teaching is unique in that you have been an apprentice in the classroom for many years. You have learned much about yourself, about good teaching, and about other people. Now students will be watching you as you transition from apprentice to master.

Your journey into the world of teaching is unique to you. It likely started very early in life. You have been a student in the classroom for over 14 years, and possibly closer to 20. During those years you have been an apprentice, observing and studying at the feet of those professionals our society has deemed worthy.

Teaching is unique in this way. What other profession lets you do a 15 year apprenticeship to help you decide whether or not you want this to be your life's work? What other profession allows you to observe both great models, and probably some poor examples, of the work that you aspire to, all before you commit yourself to the profession? In this way, deciding to become a teacher is unique. This uniqueness, if used correctly, should benefit you and make it far easier for you to master, or even excel at, your craft.

Your apprenticeship has profoundly affected you. It has impacted your daily life, your life successes, and now your life goals. It has done so consciously and unconsciously, directly and indirectly, obviously and subtly. While most, if not all, of us have reflected back on the many great teachers we have had, we need to consider a deeper analysis of the profound impact our apprenticeship has had on our decision to pursue teaching as our own life goal.

The first level of impact is obvious. It is during your apprenticeship that you learned important knowledge and skills. You learned how to read, write, do mathematics, and think critically. If you had not learned to master these basic skills, you would not be where you are today. Your first models helped you master those lessons and provided you with the foundation for all of your subsequent learning.

A second level of impact is perhaps a bit less obvious. During your apprenticeship you learned important information about yourself as a student and as a learner. You learned where your strengths and weaknesses lie, where you can excel and where you can learn to be just competent. You learned much about yourself as a student, including your own unique learning style, your ways of processing information, your own strategies for getting information into your brain, and your best ways for demonstrating that learning to others. Your knowledge in this realm is not the shared knowledge of level one. It is unique to you, and a level you must have mastered if you are going to help others gain this knowledge in the future.

Finally, a third level of impact has profoundly affected you, but you may not be as keenly aware of its influence. You observed and absorbed how others should or should not be treated, how important patience is to the learning process, how individual and cultural differences can be celebrated rather than feared, and how learning must be put into societal context to be truly understood. These were not the direct lessons of math class. These were not directly explained to you by any one teacher. Rather, these lessons have been absorbed over time, osmosing their way into your being often with little to no self-awareness.

These lessons were learned while you watched your first grade teacher struggle to help the boy next to you learn to read despite his dyslexia, while you observed your third grade teacher work to integrate the new girl who wore funny clothes into your classroom community, while you overheard your sixth grade teacher complain about students who did not do their homework, while you stood in horror as your ninth grade teacher told the boy next to you that his hands were so dirty he did not want to even touch his homework paper. The lessons and messages have been positive and negative, but always powerful. They seeped into your brain, into your being, without much, if any, awareness. They impacted who you were at the time, but more than that, they profoundly impacted who you were to become.

And finally, you learned important information about yourself. This is deep knowledge, not the surface information of your learning style and your educational strengths and weaknesses. Here you learned who you are as a person. You discovered what you prize and value in yourself and in others. Here you decided which core values will guide your life. Here you learned about what your own life priorities will be. You learned this through both intentional and unintentional reflection on the lessons learned above. You perhaps decided that your life goal will be to help the children who cannot easily learn, or perhaps to challenge and push those who have the natural ability to learn easily. You perhaps decided that teaching your students to tolerate is not sufficient, but that celebrating differences should be a goal. You perhaps decided that rewarding sound critical thinking even when you do not agree with the conclusion is a more important educational lesson than universal agreement. Whoever you have become, both as a person and as an educator, has been profoundly impacted by your apprenticeship.

In pursuing teaching as a life goal then, this is how you will impact others. Your students will be, or are, your apprentices. You are or will be the master practitioner, offering lessons to the next generation of teachers. You will affect their development and existence on all four levels. You will not simply be teaching them science or math, you will be teaching them how they learn, where they can excel, who they are as unique people, how to treat others, how to respect differences, how they can contribute to society, and what their life values and subsequent path will be. You are training and teaching those who will take your place as the natural process unfolds.

Questions for Reflection and Discussion

1. Trace your own educational history. What teachers have had a profound impact on your life? Which teachers and which experiences have impacted you at each of the four levels identified above? What do you think it was about these people, or those educational experiences, that made them so profound?
2. What do you believe about education? What do you believe about good teaching? Where did those beliefs come from? How do you put those beliefs into practice?
3. What do you hope to pass on to the next generation of apprentices? What will your legacy be?

PART II

BEING A TEACHER

In this section, you will begin to look at attitudes and attributes essential to becoming a successful teacher.

BEING AUTHENTIC

> **KEY TAKEAWAY**
>
> Be true to yourself and share yourself generously with your students. In so doing you will model the learning process for them as they become lifelong learners.

One of the best tools you have as a teacher is yourself. Skilled teachers know themselves well and use that self-knowledge to impact the learning of their students. By sharing yourself, your true self, with your students, you can help motivate them and model the learning process for them.

Being authentic is the first step in using yourself to motivate and empower learning. You simply must know yourself well, be comfortable with who you are, and then generously share yourself with your students. Students are quite in tune with how genuine and authentic you are in the classroom. They easily detect artificiality, acting, and disingenuous behavior. Likewise, they embrace genuine and authentic self-presentations. That is, it is much more important for students that you are true to yourself, that your identity in the classroom match who you are beyond the classroom, than that you act in any particular prescribed manner.

As I said, students are good diagnosticians on this issue. They will readily recognize false enthusiasm for a lesson, artificial attempts at motivation, and they will dismiss encouraging platitudes if they do not seem genuine. Moreover, the stakes are high here. If you fail here the consequences can be quick and severe, and recovery is very difficult. If you are seen as phony or fake, insincere, or even dishonest, it will be difficult for you to succeed as a successful educator. You will have undermined your message and distracted from the content of the lesson. You will have forced students to question everything you offer, whether that be a passing remark or an important piece of feedback to them. You will have lost your standing as the expert, the leader, the guide, and the helper. Recovery, if at all possible, will occur only slowly and it will have to be earned. It will be far better not to lose such standing in the first place rather than have to use valuable resources to rebuild it.

If you dedicate yourself to being genuine and honest in your self-presentation, students will forgive you for much. They can be quite understanding of your foibles and failures if you own them, rather than try to deny them. They will embrace your imperfections with you if you do not deny them in the face of reality. If organization is not your forte, do not pretend it is. If timeliness is not your strength, do not punish others for being late. If you tend to be distractible, do not excoriate the student in your class whose mind wanders. Avoiding such hypocritical displays can go a long way towards presenting yourself in this genuine and authentic manner.

Once students see you for who you are, you open a new channel of learning for them. Now you are able to motivate with your words and model with your actions. Your words become extremely powerful. Your praise of their effort or work becomes highly valued. Your critiques of their performance become believable and worthy of reflection. Your encouragement communicates to them that you truly believe that they can and will succeed. Words are no longer simply words. Words of encouragement, support, and motivation become a highly valued commodity in your classroom.

Your actions become just as, if not more, powerful than your words. Students who believe you are genuine and authentic begin to watch you more closely. Every action of yours becomes a model for them. How you handle conflict, what you find humorous, how you accept imperfections, what you tolerate, and how you communicate become the second curriculum of the classroom. You are no longer teaching simply science or history. You are teaching about life, relationships, and self-acceptance.

Soon you begin to model the entire learning process for them. They watch as you learn, as you inquire, as you study, as you research, as you struggle to comprehend, as you celebrate the joys of learning. They see that you are not perfect in your learning. Sometimes you forget, misunderstand, or miscommunicate. Sometimes you are in error. They see how you handle that. Are you defensive? Do you attack rather than acknowledge error? Or do accept your own mistakes as part of the growing process? They too will learn not to shut down after error, to see frustration as part of the learning process, and to embrace the struggles of learning if you have shown this to them.

These are essential skills for your students to learn if they are to achieve one of your primary goals for them—becoming lifelong learners. Of course you do not want their learning to stop at your classroom door. Rather, you want them to take the skills and knowledge they have acquired in your classroom out into the real world to continue the learning process. They are far more likely to do so if you have taught them more than just this theory or that fact. If you have also shown them, modeled for them, the real process of learning, along with all of its struggles and vagaries, they can then carry this forth. They are far more likely to learn this latter lesson if they watch as you genuinely demonstrate it in their classrooms and in their relationships with you.

Perhaps a word of caution could be sounded here as well. In advocating for this genuine approach, one must be careful not to blur appropriate boundaries between students and teachers. This is certainly not what is being advocated here. Being authentic does not mean you have the same relationships with everyone. Your relationships with family are different than your relationships with friends. Your relationships with students must be different than your relationships with colleagues. In all of these though, you are the common denominator. So, although your relationships may differ in actions, you remain true to yourself. You may be in a different role, but you are not a different person. At the core, you are the same person. If you pride yourself on being a fun loving and honest person, then you must be that in the classroom as well. If you are truly intense and driven, then you will be in the classroom too. Your roles in relationships change across settings, you though do not.

Questions for Reflection and Discussion

1. Where do you think you might struggle to show your authentic self to students? Why might this be? Do you think this is something you might want to improve on? How might you go about doing so?
2. What are the limits on your being authentic and genuine in your interactions with students? Where might some danger points lie if you are not careful?
3. If you had to define yourself in one sentence, what would that sentence be? How do you stay true to that definition in the classroom and in your interactions with students?

BEING PASSIONATE

KEY TAKEAWAY

No doubt you are a passionate learner. Pass that passion on to your students and you will have given them a gift they will use throughout their lives.

You simply must teach from passion. Your passion is no doubt multifaceted. You likely have a passion for your discipline. Whether it be social studies, mathematics, literature, or psychology, you love your discipline. If you want to be an excellent teacher you must also have a passion for the craft of teaching. Challenging yourself to improve as a teacher is often the core sign of a truly passionate teacher. And finally, you likely have a general passion for learning. It is this last passion that you will be able to communicate and pass on to your students.

I do not think that this passion can be created. Most likely, it already resides within you. This passion is an insatiable, and realistically, irrational love. It is what drives your study. It supports and re-energizes you at those times when frustrations, and even despair, creep in. It can lay dormant for years and emerge later in life, but it cannot be created artificially. To be an excellent teacher this passion must be centered in three areas: the discipline in which you teach; the craft of teaching itself; and the joy of learning in general.

This passion for your discipline is first for you, only later to be shared with your students. It nourishes you, and you must nourish it back. It will later form the foundation for the passion and zeal you model for your students, but at the start it is yours to guard selfishly. And you must guard it. Many will want to diminish it, deprive you of it, even negate it. You will be, or have been, told that it is foolish, that you must be more practical, that you cannot spend all of your time doing this, that the real world beckons, and that you must grow up. You are no doubt by now practiced at resisting the power of these arguments and even counterbalancing them with better logic. You will need to keep up that practice as the assault on your passion is not likely to diminish.

You know what your passion is. It is that thing you do when you have your choice of activities. It is that thing you do when you really should be doing something else. It is the thing you want to talk to others about, no matter what the time or place. It is the thing that allows you to lose track of time, to be engrossed, to "flow" as Mihaly

Csikszentmihalyi (1990) calls it. You have nurtured it throughout your life and now, as a teacher, it is time to share it.

Having that passion, though, is not enough to make you a good teacher. You must also have a passion to share it. And this sharing cannot be on your terms, it must be on the terms of the receiver, the student. That is, if you are to be a successful teacher you must have a passion for sharing your knowledge. This passion for the craft of teaching must become your second, or even your primary passion, if you are to be successful.

Once again you must nurture this second passion. You must feed it the same way you have fed your primary passion. You must live it, discuss it, analyze it, read about it, listen to others who share this passion, and even debate those who call your passion silly. It will not grow without this. It will not disappear, but it will wither in response to its neglect.

It is a third passion, however, that may be most influential in the classroom. Part of a good teacher's passion is grounded in neither her discipline nor her love of teaching. Rather, a healthy part of her passion lies in a passionate quest for all knowledge. The excitement of learning, and learning throughout a lifetime, is something that is apparent in almost all good teachers. In fact it is this aspect of passion that is contagiously caught by students.

Your passion for your discipline allows you to invest the necessary energy needed to learn deeply but narrowly. Your passion for teaching drives your quest for new strategies and techniques that will allow you to reach more students more effectively. But it is your general passion for learning that students will notice and copy. And there are numerous things you can do to make sure they get the lesson.

You must model this passion for them. First, you must communicate to them that learning is inherently good, and that not knowing something is an opportunity, not a flaw of character. It may be reflective of missed or unavailable opportunities, or simply chances that have not yet arisen. Having the chance to learn anything is a privilege and your attitude towards things you do not know will either support or undermine that message.

Second you must model for them that learning does not end at the end of this class, at the end of this grade, or semester, or year. Rather learning is a lifelong process that you yourself are still committed to, energized and excited by, and hungry for. Part of your class must demonstrate this. Your entire class cannot be simply shifting knowledge from your repository to theirs. Part of class must be an exploration for both of you. It must allow them to learn new things, that is things that may be new to you as well.

Moreover, you must show them regularly that you welcome that learning. You must model the curiosity that always drives new learning. You must ask them to teach you about things, letting them be the expert, the teacher, the model. And simultaneously you must be the novice, the student, but always the model. They may not be able to teach you anything about your discipline; they may or may not be able to teach you anything about good teaching; but they can teach you about their

16

world, their culture, their areas of passion. In so doing you have nurtured both their specific passion and your own passion for learning.

Third, give permission to yourself, and to them, not to know everything. Encourage them to ask you questions that go beyond the lesson. Share your knowledge with them if you know the answer, but more importantly join with them in figuring out answers to questions you do not know. Publicly declare when you do not know the answers to their questions, rather than hiding behind excuses and rationalizations. Students will not see such openness as weakness or ignorance; they will see it for exactly what it is—honesty about the process of learning.

Ask them questions that encourage them to think beyond their current knowledge. In so doing, though, respect the process of learning. Understand that you are pushing them beyond their comfort zone, and accord them the same safe environment to search for an answer that you would benefit from. These challenging questions cannot be an expression and reflection of your power; they must be genuine attempts to push the search for knowledge.

You owe it to yourself and your students to make public your passions. Private passions can fulfill you, but will not likely impact the lives of others. Teachers are passionate about impacting the lives of others. Whether your students catch your passion for your discipline, for teaching, or simply for learning, you will have done them a wonderful service by sharing all three passions with them.

Questions for Reflection and Discussion

1. Where do your passions lie? What do you love to learn about?
2. How do you demonstrate your passion for learning in everyday life?
3. What types of classroom activities or interactions can help instill a passion for learning in students? What types of activities or interactions might work against that goal?

BEING ZEALOUS

KEY TAKEAWAY

Teach with intensity and enthusiasm. Your energy will make your passion for learning come to life. Your zeal will be contagious.

John Baptiste de La Salle was born into a wealthy French family in the mid 1600's. Early in life he abandoned his wealth to devote himself to educating children who were less fortunate than he. De La Salle organized a group of lay teachers who shared his devotion to education and established a Roman Catholic order of Brothers devoted to education. This order, now known as the Christian Brothers, continues to educate millions worldwide through their network of high schools and colleges (Lasallian Heritage--St. John Baptiste De La Salle, 2012). De La Salle was a pioneer in more than just organization; he was a pioneer in understanding the process of excellent teaching. Through his writings and those of his followers, students continue to study his observations and suggestions for excellence in teaching and education. One of De La Salle's twelve tenets for teaching excellence was to teach with "zeal" (Agathon, as translated by Rummery, 1998). Though far ahead of his time, this advice is still essential today.

But what exactly is "zeal?" I think zeal is best understood as the combination of intensity and enthusiasm. Although the term "zealot" has negative connotations today, a zealous commitment to teaching excellence and a zealous approach in the classroom are likely to produce quite positive results in learning.

In many ways zeal can be seen as a complement to the passion described in the previous chapter. The passion a great teacher has for the educational process must be communicated to the student. Without this communication, the passion may continue to drive the instructor, but will not transfer the hunger for learning to the student. It is zeal that allows for that transfer. It is zeal that communicates your internal passion to the hungry student.

Zealous teaching is intense and energetic. It is enthusiastic and demanding. It is active and challenging. It is the direct reflection of the passion for learning that burns within.

A zealous teacher is easily recognizable. Her classroom is energized. It exudes excitement. There is little place for passivity in this classroom. Time is not wasted; rather it is a precious asset which often runs low.

Despite this level of energy, this classroom is not chaotic or disorganized. In fact, it might be said that it is "hyperfocused." The students and the teacher are hyperfocused on learning. The learning focus though is not narrow. Any and all learning is fair game. While the main learning goal will be crystal clear, the voracious appetite to learn may also ensnare secondary learning opportunities. Unanticipated opportunities to teach about related, or even only semi-related topics, must be seized. Almost any learning opportunity is a good learning opportunity. Theorists and practitioners talk about "teachable moments." The teacher committed to teaching with zeal finds teachable moments everywhere, and seizes them.

This hyperfocus on learning is directly communicated to students on a regular basis. Students are not left to discover this strategy on their own. The zealous teacher explains to them that learning is everything, that we cannot let anything get in the way of learning in this classroom, and that together we must commit ourselves 100 percent to the process of learning. This explanation is verbal, direct, and frequent. Thus, all activities must share this hyperfocus. There can be no busywork, no assignment where students do not understand how it contributes to the learning process. Even activities that involve assessing learning, like exams or projects, can be an opportunity for learning. The connections between all activities and learning must be explicit.

Students will only buy into your zealous commitment to learning if you are consistent and genuine. If your energy varies significantly by the day, if your assignments seem to them only tangentially related to the lessons or of questionable importance, if you seem more interested in something else, anything else, beyond their learning in the moment, they will not accompany you on this exciting journey. This can be a daunting and exhausting ride that will emerge out of your own genuine desire to learn and to teach.

You may be wondering about how anyone could maintain this necessary level of energy. It is truly a curious thing. Truly zealous teaching is in fact energizing rather than depleting. Simply playing the role or acting the part of zealous teacher would in fact be too exhausting. That level of intensity and enthusiasm, when not genuine, would drain you quickly. When it is genuine and thus met by receptive learners, it tends to grow rather than shrink, empower rather than weaken, embolden rather than deflate, invigorate rather than deplete. The zealous teacher leaves the classroom disappointed that time has run out, that there is no more room for learning today. The zealous teacher leaves the room without realizing that she is "spent." That exhausted feeling does not come until later when the energy of the teaching moment is no longer immediately present.

In the zealous teacher's classroom the energy is contagious. Students catch it from the teacher, but then it takes on a life of its own. Students pass it on to each other. And it is not bound by the four physical walls of the classroom. It moves into the hallways, the lunchroom, the dormitory rooms, or the family dinner table. It is a powerful process, potent enough to even infect people who never personally set foot in your classroom.

De La Salle's emphasis on zeal is highly instructive for all teachers, no matter their discipline or their beliefs. While having passion may energize you, teaching with zeal energizes both you and the student. Zeal becomes the energy for current learning and the catalyst for the student's future study.

Questions for Reflection and Discussion

1. What do you have zeal for and how do you demonstrate it? How is your demonstration unique to who you are as a person?
2. Can you identify a teacher you have had who taught with zeal? What impact did that person have on your life and your learning? Can you see how his or her zeal might have spread well beyond the four walls of the classroom?
3. How can a lack of zeal in the classroom impact student learning?

BEING GREEDY

KEY TAKEAWAY

When it comes to expectations for your students' learning, greed is good. Have high expectations, communicate them directly and indirectly, and always believe that potential can be realized.

We usually do not think that greed is good. In fact, tradition suggests that it is one of the seven deadly sins. When it comes to learning expectations for our students, though, perhaps greed is in fact good.

As a teacher, you should never be satisfied with the extent of your students' learning. There is always more to learn, new ways to understand, novel applications, and creative analyses. Just as you are never satisfied with your own learning, you should not be satisfied with your students' learning. While lessons certainly must start at whatever point your learners are at, this limitation does not define how far you can eventually go. Simply because you might have to start at a very basic level, this should not limit your expectations.

It is best to communicate this to students both directly and indirectly. The direct message is simple—I want you to learn as much as possible. I even use the term "greedy" when I discuss this with my classes. I explain to them that I believe they have much potential, that they can achieve great things, and that I am going to be "greedy" about their learning. Therefore I set high but achievable goals for them and encourage them to embrace them with me. Throughout the academic term I make reference to my greed, with hopes that they too will begin to be greedy about their own learning and expectations.

This must also be communicated indirectly. One indirect way in which you communicate this is in how you use your classroom time. Classroom time is a very limited resource and you must maximize its usage. Wasting time in class is an indirect message to your students that you do not believe they can learn. This is a devastating message and will likely undermine all of your otherwise good intentions. Therefore, class time should be held sacred, with lesson plans designed to productively use all of the time allotted. Some of the best teachers begin educating before the bell rings and even express their frustration as students pack their bags after the dismissal time has passed.

Assignments are a second way you communicate your expectations to your students. If you only give assignments that students can easily complete, what message are you giving them? Are you not saying that you think that this is the only level they can handle? Certainly you do not want to communicate that. After all, you do not even know the answer to how much each of your students might be able to learn.

Rather you want to use assignments that reinforce and spur further learning. Assignments that have two components to them are often quite useful. Component one might be questions or problems that review the specifics of the current or past lessons. These are designed to allow for practice and to demonstrate mastery, and likely will constitute the majority of assignments. Component two, however, pushes students beyond the limits of the classroom lesson. Component two pushes students to solve novel problems, apply concepts in new ways, or apply lessons to new situations. These are the "challenge" problems, but they should not be reserved for just the best students or the honors classes. Rather, everyone should be challenged to some degree.

Grading assignments gives you yet another opportunity to spur your students on to even deeper learning. While a number grade may objectively capture the percentage of questions a student answered correctly, its message is limited. Complementing that number grade with three simple sentences can continue to push students beyond their current learning. A first sentence in which you translate that number into words for them can be helpful. A grade of "B" translates into a "good job." A grade of "C" translates into an "average job." For some students using the evaluative word can push them more than the number alone. A second sentence in which you quickly explain how the assignment could have been improved suggests a path to higher achievement. For example, a grade of 85% might be complemented with the simple sentences "You did a good job on this assignment. Pushing this to the next level would have involved...."

It is the third sentence, though, that really communicates your expectations, hopes, and your greed. Here is where you challenge the student to apply the concept to a new area. It can often be posed as an invitation for further thinking and conversation. For example, you might write "We should discuss how you think the author of this novel might have better reached today's audience." Or you might say, "We should talk about how you might apply this physics concept to how roller coasters are designed." Any topic can lend itself to this type of challenge. It must, however, invite the student to consider an application to an area he or she might be naturally interested in. Otherwise it is far too easily dismissed.

Most importantly, though, you must follow up on these final challenging comments. Asking the student after class as to his or her thoughts on the topic can remind the student that you wanted to have a deeper discussion with him. Raising it in class can be effective as well, as other students then gain the benefit of everyone else's challenge questions. In either case the message is clear—that I believe you can understand this concept deeply enough for it to be meaningful to you and helpful to others.

Sometimes the payoff for your greed does not come immediately. It often sits quietly within a student, sometimes even for years. Even then though the message that you believe the student can learn and contribute has been communicated. Its dormancy might last days, weeks, months or years. Sadly we are often not around when it awakens, but it often does. And then there is significant payoff for the student.

Communicate your greed for your students' learning. It is one of your long term gifts to your students.

Questions for Reflection and Discussion

1. Take any assignment and redesign it so that it has both a mastery and a challenge component to it. Consider how difficult that process was. Where did you struggle? How might you improve your ability on this skill?
2. Think back to your own education. What teachers did you have who were greedy about your learning? How did they communicate that to you? Were you aware of it at the time? When did you realize the message that they were giving to you?
3. Can you think of other ways to communicate greed for learning to students?

BEING MORE THAN TOLERANT: CELEBRATING DIFFERENCES

KEY TAKEAWAY

Every student you will teach will be unique. Tolerating different cultural backgrounds, learning styles, levels of motivation, and other aspects that make each of us unique is essential to good teaching. Celebrating and building on those differences make for great teaching.

Tolerance is an essential quality for a successful teacher. There are four particular areas in which a good teacher must demonstrate tolerance: tolerance of cultural differences; tolerance of divergent thinking and opinion; tolerance of learning styles; and tolerance of individual differences.

"Tolerant" or "tolerance" is an important word here. To be tolerant of something is to accept it without feeling the need to change it. To be tolerant of something is to work within its context and its boundaries. To be tolerant of something is to show respect for it.

But is tolerance enough? Tolerance often connotes the idea that while we don't agree, we have respect for other viewpoints and experiences. Demonstrating this respect is certainly a minimum in any good classroom. Celebrating those differences though may differentiate the good classroom from the great one.

Celebrating culture, then, refers to the idea that teachers go beyond simple understanding and appreciation of cultural differences. They go beyond simply being tolerant of such differences. Each student arrives in your classroom with a cultural heritage and history. None of them asked for that baggage or blessing; it came with their birth and their subsequent life history. They no more could control those experiences than determine their eye color.

Thus, it makes little sense for you as a teacher to ask students to work within your culture. They do not, and sometimes will not, understand your cultural context. It makes far more sense for you to understand their culture, to celebrate it, and to try to build a bridge between yours and theirs. It is this bridge that you must both traverse together, although you will not be able to meet halfway. You will have to meet closer to the other side if you are to be successful.

Cultural differences will come into play in a variety of places and manners in the classroom. Four manifestations of culture are particularly important to pay attention to in the classroom as they will impact a wide variety of classroom activities and experiences. These four components include personal space, eye contact, physical contact, and communication style (Hays & McLeod, 2010).

Some cultures are accustomed to close personal proximities, and in fact only feel comfortable communicating in such tight quarters. Others demand more space. This is important to understand and plan for in a classroom. Seating arrangements and group activities can be significantly impacted by this cultural difference.

Eye contact is another common cultural difference (Hays & McLeod, 2010; Garrett, 2010). For some cultures it is considered disrespectful for a student or younger person to make direct eye contact with a teacher or elder. In sharp contrast to this are cultures which insist on direct eye contact as a core social skill.

Physical contact is also commonly misunderstood. Just as with eye contact, physical contact means different things in different cultures (Hays & McLeod, 2010). The same action can be interpreted as a sign of affection or aggression, of friendliness or boundary crossing. In almost all cases physical contact is a powerful message. Know what message you are delivering and how it will be perceived.

We all have different styles of communication (Hays & McLeod, 2010; Helm & James, 2010). While these are idiosyncratic to our personalities, there are strong cultural contributions to these styles. Some cultures communicate very directly, even endorsing direct challenge. Others are far more indirect, doing almost everything to avoid direct exchange. Some speak openly about feelings, while for others feelings are consistently avoided. Of course so much of what goes on in the classroom is communication. It is verbal and nonverbal in nature. It is direct and indirect. It would be almost impossible to construct a competent lesson plan without understanding the cultural communication patterns of your students.

These cultural issues play out most clearly in two educational activities. The first is group work. Students will respond to group work quite differently, in part dependent upon their cultural heritage (Gladding, 2012). First, for many students, group work is difficult to adapt to. Some societies and cultures tend to be individualistic by tradition, if not by nature. Interestingly, American culture is one of these. In contrast, other cultures are more collectivistic (Hays & McLeod, 2010; Helm & James, 2010). Students who have been raised in more collectivistic cultures are likely to take to group work more readily. Those raised to be individuals, sometimes even to the cost of the group, struggle in such activities. In these latter cases, group work often deteriorates into modified individual work, thus defeating the planned benefits of learning to work in a cooperative manner and depriving everyone of the synergistic benefits of learning together.

Second, we often try to encourage our students to question and challenge. We push them to ask important questions, challenge experts, and even wonder about commonly held beliefs. We see these as the hallmarks of good students and often as central to the learning process. This skill of questioning, however, does run counter to many cultural teachings and traditions. Many students are raised to think that such questioning is disrespectful, especially when directed at older individuals or individuals society has deemed experts. Here the cultural push to observe, follow, and accept is being challenged. While this can also produce excellent learning results in certain circumstances, it is not what we urge our students to learn to do as we teach critical thinking and liberal education to them. It is important to remember that this skill will be difficult for some students to accept as important, and thus to learn.

Your appreciation for these cultural differences here will understandably limit you. At times it will restrict your manner of teaching, the types of assignments you give, and even essential relationship building with your students. But, in essence, you have no choice. Social workers have a wonderful saying that one needs to "meet her client where she is at." Educators might adapt this to the classroom; you must accept your students for who they are. You cannot teach them as if they are who you would like them to be.

You cannot become an effective teacher without understanding the cultural influences in your students' lives. These influences will impact their learning behaviors both in and outside of the classroom, their motivation to learn and succeed academically, how their academic success will be interpreted and respected, and how those academic lessons might be used in the future. Understanding these cultural influences, and then using that knowledge to more effectively plan and implement lessons, will improve your teaching effectiveness.

You must be at least tolerant of, and hopefully celebrate, other differences beyond culture as well. You must appreciate different learning styles. Other essays address the issue of learning styles in depth, and that is not the focus here. Rather, again, accepting and appreciating these differences is essential to success, yours and thus theirs.

Students who are auditory learners will likely always be auditory learners. Those who learn primarily experientially will continue to do so. While it certainly would be easier if all of your students' learning styles matched yours, or matched your primary modality of teaching, this simply will not be the case. Wishing it so will certainly not make it so. Instead, you must accept these learning style differences.

This has very practical ramifications for your teaching. You simply cannot teach through only one stylistic modality. You must use multiple modalities. Each lesson must be presented through multiple learning channels if you are going to connect with all of your students. It is not realistic, fair, or acceptable to teach in only way. This is disrespectful to all of the students who learn differently. It gives the authoritarian message that you will learn my way simply because I said so. Of course such teaching is doomed for failure.

While you must understand stylistic differences in thinking, tolerance of the content of thought is just as important. You must tolerate thoughts and opinions which differ from your own. Academe is the place, and perhaps one of the only places left, where challenging and controversial ideas can be aired, tested, debated, and researched. In essence, this is the golden goal of education. School is not the place where students simply memorize lessons or have their thinking programmed. It is the place where they learn to think for themselves. They cannot possibly learn this most valuable of lessons unless you, as their teacher, celebrate challenges to your own ideas. If you rigidly expect your students to follow your lead, you are not educating them, you are training them. Celebrating diverse and divergent thought is essential for true education.

Finally, you must be appreciative of individual differences. Psychologists love to talk about individual differences. The idea behind individual differences is a basic one. No matter how well we might categorize, classify, group, or even diagnose people, there are significant individual differences that supersede such organizational efforts. Not all women think alike; each African American student, despite sharing an ethnicity, learns differently; each student with a learning disability processes the world uniquely. In essence, we are all unique learners who fit into multiple groups, but those groups can only explain a part of our identity. Another part of who we are remains idiosyncratic to each of us as unique human beings.

Successful teachers are always looking for the keys to a student's mind (Levine, 2002). While some keys fit many minds, each of our minds has a special key pressed just for it. Individual differences force excellent teachers to carry key rings, rather than a simple master key. Much of the job of the excellent teacher is learning which key might fit which student's mind, and even pressing new keys when tried and true ones fail.

Tolerating, and even celebrating, these differences is essential to successful teaching. In teaching, celebrating means far more than acceptance. It involves prizing the individual for his uniqueness, understanding that his particular uniqueness was not designed or requested by him, and creatively developing lessons that can effectively open that student's mind to the pleasure and power of learning.

Questions for Reflection and Discussion

1. What other "tolerances" might a successful teacher need to develop and demonstrate? Why are those tolerances important to the learning process? How might a teacher make sure that she develops such tolerances?
2. Can you learn to appreciate and celebrate differences? What limits us in these realms? What can we do to improve ourselves in this realm?
3. Think about the concept of culture broadly. What aspects of your cultural background, outside of ethnicity, are likely to impact your teaching? In what ways will these things impact your teaching?

PART III

CLASSROOM CULTURE

In this section you will begin to examine what happens inside the classroom. You will be challenged to examine how teachers create successful classrooms.

EARNING RESPECT

KEY TAKEAWAY

Respect needs to be earned. It develops in a fair, consistent, strength-oriented classroom that prizes each individual student. It should be directly and indirectly addressed in the classroom.

Respect is a commodity that needs to be earned, not simply demanded and subsequently granted. Earned respect is strong and enduring. True it builds slowly and gradually, but once rooted, it is difficult to displace. It is the plant with deep roots. Stresses have little impact on it. This type of respect withstands the vagaries of relationships, the natural ebbs and flows of life, and even the frontal assault of significant trauma. This is the type of respect you want to build with your students as this is the only type of respect strong enough to last.

Respect is earned in both the big and little occurrences in the classroom. It cannot be earned through one grand gesture or one good week. It must build over time. In many ways, it is like a plant growing from a seed. When tended well, the seed develops roots deep into the soil. The roots are not visible to the naked eye as they are beneath the dirt. One must assume their development as a matter of faith until the seedling sprouts one day, often unexpectedly, from the ground. This is what respect looks like in its earliest days. It is buried under the everyday clamor of the classroom, the din of discussion, and the urgency of assignments. All the while though it can be growing and developing, laying down roots that will allow it to be resilient in times of stress.

As that seed emerges from the ground, it begins to grow. It needs sunlight and water to thrive. It must be tended to, but not smothered. Respect too needs care and space. As the respect in the classroom emerges, it still must be fed with further acts of understanding and empathy, in combination with reasonable demands and expectations.

Eventually that plant can stand on its own. Its roots are deep and its stem is strong. Environmental stresses are inconsequential to its continued growth, as long as not too severe. And soon its growth rate is remarkable. The tiny plant that seemed fragile just a few weeks ago has doubled or tripled in size. Its growth rate has become geometric, seemingly adding inches overnight. It can stand on its own now. It only needs protection from the catastrophic acts of nature. The respect that you planted in the classroom has also sprouted. It too has developed deep roots and a strong constitution. It no longer needs the constant tending it did at the start. It will now survive the ordinary stresses of life. Care now must be taken simply to avoid the catastrophic, the traumatic, failure.

To demand respect without earning it is akin to expecting this plant to grow and withstand stress despite having a very shallow, or even no, root system. It will look sturdy and attractive, until it is stressed. However, as soon as that strong wind blows through, as soon as it is truly stressed, it will become uprooted or break off, leaving it dead in the dirt.

Once philosophically committed to the idea that respect is essential in the classroom and that it must be grown rather than demanded, there are many ways to plant, nurture, support, and protect its development. The first requirement is that the topic of respect becomes an explicit part of your classroom conversations. Therefore, the very first step is to help your students understand what respect is and what it looks like. You cannot expect them to learn and later demonstrate it, if they do not even recognize it. Defining the term, explaining it in developmentally appropriate words, and giving examples are good first steps. Labeling it when you see it, pointing it out when you or others do it, and recognizing it in the content lessons of the classroom can all be first steps in the growing process. Whether you are teaching third graders or college students, no assumption should be made that it will appear on its own. By introducing the topic you are planting the seed.

Once planted, it must be tended to. There are four guidelines to consider in caring for this new seed. First is fairness. Respect develops out of fairness. Disrespect emerges from inequities. People, even younger children, often have an innate sense of fairness. We feel it in our own relationships and take notice of it in the relationships around us. We bristle when we experience its failure. Even though we might not call attention to its presence, or even its absence, it is noted. A relationship built on fairness has the chance of growing into respect. Respect will never emerge if injustice characterizes the relationship.

Second is consistency. Consistency here refers to consistency to oneself, not blind rule following. Relationships with others are always highly variable. You cannot treat everyone exactly the same way. Different people need different things from you. But you must be consistent to who you are. You cannot one day value hard work and the next value only high achievement. You cannot today praise class participation and tomorrow denigrate an unsolicited comment. You must be confident and comfortable in who you are, and consistent in your behaviors that emerge from that identity. The seed cannot one day be watered excessively, only to be neglected for weeks following. It must be tended to everyday, especially in those early times, with the same consistent care.

A third guideline for building respect involves focusing on your students' strengths rather than simply attacking weaknesses. Clearly communicating what you see as a student's strengths and how that might be nurtured and developed can be powerful. Simply hearing strengths articulated aloud can be empowering. Moreover, calling attention to personal achievement can be transformational. A student moving from a grade of "C" to a grade of "B" has accomplished much. Sometimes that accomplishment is greater than the student maintaining the "A" level of achievement that comes naturally to him. Recognizing strengths and achievements is powerful. Moreover, it is too early to attack weaknesses. You need your plant's roots to be stronger before you stress them.

Fourth, you cannot fall trap to valuing people because of their academic achievements. Academic achievement must be separated from the prizing of the student as a human being. Every student deserves attention, care, instruction, and respect. The "A" student is not more worthy than the "C" student. True she has achieved to higher degree, but only in this narrow academic realm. She is not a better person and not deserving of superior respect. This is an area in which you must watch your subtle communications. When you spend more time praising the "A" student, you are delivering a message to those who did not achieve at this level. This message is disempowering and destructive. It says "You are not as worthy of my attention." While most, if not all, of us would never plan to distribute our attention, care, and respect based on academic achievement, accidently we sometimes communicate exactly this in our classrooms.

Really only one thing must be assiduously avoided in this process of building and earning respect—personal attacks. Respect will never develop out of such behavior. Fear might emerge, and for a short time it might look like respect, but it is nothing like respect. Fear is reactive, it is only temporarily energizing, and it dissipates when its source is gone. It is not relationship based; it is situationally based.

The tearing down of the individual by definition is a destructive act. The building of respect is a constructive act. It is this construction that will support your students in stressful times. Experiences of destruction leave you impotent when the inevitable stresses of life appear on your doorstep. As such, fear has no place in the classroom.

Your classroom culture of respect will not survive major trauma either. Demonstrations of gross disrespect and severe relationship failures constitute such trauma and are strong enough to destroy the plant you have nurtured. You must carefully avoid such traumatic experiences since once occurring it becomes difficult if not impossible to regenerate the level of respect you had cultivated. The strong plant that is even accidentally uprooted by the summer storm rarely thrives again.

Granted, your plant will still need some tending and care. Small unhealthy patterns of behavior will have crept into your classroom and begun to steal your attention and energy. At these times a simple weeding should suffice. A revisiting of the topic of respect, a recommitment to fairness and personal consistency, and a refocus on strengths should get your classroom community back on track.

By modeling respect towards your students in the classroom, the culture of respect will grow. Students will demonstrate respect towards themselves, their peers, and you. This culture will grow slowly at first, but its acceleration will astound you. If cultivated correctly, one day you will stand back and observe its unprompted existence and demonstration. You will marvel at how strong your plant has become and how little it needs you now.

Questions for Reflection and Discussion

1. Do you tend to demand respect in your relationships, or do you work to earn it? Why do we tend to demand it before we have earned it?
2. What things do you specifically do to support, or undermine, the process of earning respect in your relationships? What types of things might constitute the "severe relationship failures" that almost inevitably destroy respect?
3. Consider the grade level you teach or hope to teach. What specific behaviors and activities might you engage in within the classroom to help build a culture of respect?

ESTABLISHING RULES

KEY TAKEAWAY

The key classroom rule is simply this: no one is allowed to interfere with anyone else's learning. Stay focused on this core rule and you will be able to commit to your main job, helping students learn. Use your creativity to design lessons that engage students and that leave them little time to create problems.

The issue of classroom rules cuts across all levels of teaching. Granted teachers at varying levels face slightly different challenges, but the general behavioral goals are the same. Teachers want students to be honest, respectful, and focused on learning. While the enforcement strategies might differ somewhat depending upon the developmental level of the students, the goals really remain the same.

Some teachers get distracted from their primary purpose by the issue of rules. That is, the establishment of rules, and their subsequent enforcement, become the educational focus. This is terribly problematic for one primary reason. You can only have one clear focus in the classroom, and that focus must be on learning. If your attention is divided between learning and rules, you are taking very valuable time away from the teaching process and stacking the deck against both yourself and your students.

It is usually obvious as this destructive process unfolds. More and more time is spent in class discussing rules and consequences, and less time is spent teaching. More and more time outside of class is spent thinking about behavior management, classroom control, and cheating than actual lesson planning. More and more time is spent in conversations with colleagues complaining about students, their lack of respect, and ways in which to ensure that they are not cheating. Sometimes teachers become consumed by this issue. As a result their teaching naturally suffers.

Not coincidentally, it is usually at this time that the teacher becomes increasingly disenchanted with her job. Complaining about students increases and the burn out process accelerates. Unfortunately this is easily noticed by the students as well. They quickly realize that you are disenchanted and increasingly disengaged. This usually worsens the behavior management issues and a very vicious cycle has been established.

While it would be impossible to address every possible behavior problem and potential intervention across the various levels of education, a general approach should be strongly considered as it can address the vast majority of real and potential problems. This approach involves emphasizing just two simple rules in the classroom, regardless of academic level. These two rules are broad enough to encompass most student problems. By addressing the issue on this general level, you free your time and energy to focus on your real goal—student learning.

Rule number one is simply this: You are not allowed to do anything that interferes with anyone else's learning. It is remarkable how broad but powerful this simple rule really is. It is based on the foundation of respect, but specific enough to allow for clear application. It is something that students of all ages can understand and appreciate. Second graders and college students will endorse its basic fairness and its simplicity.

The third grader who is talking to her neighbor, the fifth grader who is shooting spitballs, the seventh grader who is making obscene gestures, the high schooler who is making smart-aleck comments, and the college student seated in the middle of the room who is surfing the internet on his laptop are all interfering with other students' learning. Everyone would agree that this is not acceptable. If students understand from minute one that this is the lens through which you will judge their behavior, long explanations and discussions as to why behaviors are inappropriate become unnecessary. You either are or are not interfering with other students' learning.

No investigation is needed. No long conversations are warranted. No additional time spent away from the lesson is wasted. Your expectation is clear. The consequence of course will depend upon your setting, but even this becomes simpler with the application of this one dimensional rule.

Of course then you must become comfortable with the limitations of this rule. Certain actions may no longer be considered simply behavioral issues. For example the student sleeping in your class may no longer really be a behavior problem. Nor is the college student sitting in the back silently texting during your lecture. These are now simply students whom you have not yet fully engaged in the learning activity of the day. Of course this puts the burden back on you. Their failure may now really be your failure. But in fact this may be a fair assessment. While it may be that they are simply tired from working too many hours, exhausted from listening to the constant fighting in their home, or simply completely uninterested in the topic at hand, it also may be that they remain candidates to become engaged in learning if you can find a way to stimulate their motivation.

This is not to say that you should ignore these "problems." Rather, this suggests that you view these problems through a different lens—the lens of teaching rather than the lens of behavior management. The goal then becomes engagement rather than control. Devising lessons that force task involvement and investment is often your best strategy in managing such off task behaviors.

Rule number two is simply this: Be honest. Honesty here includes not cheating and admitting your mistakes. Many times teachers spend inordinate amounts of time defining cheating, trying to prevent cheating, investigating cheating, and responding to cheating. This is time that could be much better spent in the classroom or in lesson preparation. In many ways it is wasted time and energy.

It is fairly easy to manage and apply this rule in the classroom. First of all, since honesty goes far beyond simply not cheating, a culture of honesty must be established. It must be talked about directly at the start of the term. It must be modeled by you. This modeling is probably best accomplished through your acknowledgment of your own mistakes. Modeling how to admit mistakes and modeling the fact that you are less than perfect diffuses one of the two main reasons for cheating. Most cheating is done because students are either afraid of appearing incompetent or because their personality structure leads them to cut corners and be dishonest. There is not much you can do about the latter condition, even if you focused on it every day in your classroom. It is inherent to that individual; it has nothing to do with the milieu of your classroom. Modeling mistakes and tolerance however will decrease the motivation to cheat in students who were originally well intentioned. This preventive step can be very effective.

Cheating can also be discouraged through well planned assignments. Assignments can be created that are almost "cheat-proof." Of course, in reality no assignment is completely cheat proof, but certainly some are better than others. For example, assignments that ask students to apply learning to their own lives are difficult to steal from others. Assignments that ask students for their own analyses, that rely on data you provide for them, that ask them to analyze specific arguments, that include collecting their own data, or that involve creative works are all difficult to copy or fabricate.

In essence, you need all of your time and energy to implement excellent lessons. Time spent on behavior is lost time. Moreover, when it becomes the focus, the educational battle is lost.

Questions for Reflection and Discussion

1. Picture the grade level you hope to, or are currently, teaching. What simple things might you do at the start of the year to help ensure that as little time as possible is squandered on behavioral issues?
2. Again, picture the grade level you hope to be, or are currently, teaching. In what ways do students of this age interfere with other students' learning? How might you structure assignments and class activities in order to minimize these distractions?
3. Why do you think some teachers become almost obsessed with the issues of behavior management and cheating? What effect do you think this has on their teaching? Knowing yourself well, what steps might you take to guard against this?

APPRECIATING GROUP PROCESSES AND DYNAMICS

KEY TAKEAWAY

A class is a group of students. As such, group dynamics rules apply. A good teacher is knowledgeable about group dynamics and processes, monitors group development, rules, and roles, and teaches students how to be good group members.

A class of students is a group. As such, it is subject to all we know about group dynamics. It would be impossible to address even a small fraction of the complex issue of group dynamics in the classroom within a brief essay, but a few thoughts are certainly warranted. I want to simply mention two aspects of group dynamics to think about as it relates to the classroom, with the clear understanding that we are not even scratching the surface of this important topic. Perhaps such thoughts will encourage you to undertake a more thorough study of the topic by reviewing and considering some important readings and theories.

One of the most important aspects of a group to pay attention to is its norms or rules (Gladding, 2012). Each group has both explicit and implicit norms, and the skilled teacher is involved in establishing and monitoring both. On an explicit level, these norms constitute the basic rules of the classroom. Obviously these should be well thought out and clearly articulated to students. In Chapter 9 we talked about these classroom rules. The essence of that chapter was this: Focusing excessively on classroom rules distracts you from your main goal of teaching. An overarching rule that prohibits students from interfering in any way with other students' learning is a good general guideline.

Norms though are often implicit as well. The implicit norms often have roots in the past and get modified by present experiences. In almost all cases, your students will have been in other classrooms before yours. They will have learned rules, and less formal ways of operating, there. They will have observed the implied norms of many classrooms and they bring that knowledge and experience to your classroom. This can be either, or both, a good and bad thing. These historical norms will become the foundation upon which the norms of your classroom are built. If your norms complement the students' experiences, it will be an easy fit. If they do not, it will be an adjustment. As a teacher you must be very aware of this. If your style of teaching is very different from that commonly experienced by your students, they will struggle with their overall adjustment at the start. More explicit norms related specifically to your style may be necessary then to help them make the transition.

You must pay attention to norms throughout the life of your class. They are dynamic, not static, and the skilled teacher keeps her finger on their pulse. It is easy to track the explicit rules of your classroom, but the implied norms must be monitored carefully. Are there subtle messages, either constructive or destructive, that are being shared amongst students? What are these messages? Are they helping to build a learning community or interfering with that process? Are they empowering learning or distracting the group from the process? Pay careful attention here. It is often a group's implicit norms that influence its success.

Let's look at an example here. Sometimes a group develops a norm that it is unacceptable to work hard. Diligence is looked at askance and may even be openly mocked. This is tremendously problematic for the teacher who is trying to build an industrious classroom community. This type of implicit norm must be recognized early, and changed.

It is also important to remember that members of groups have different roles, and this diversity is important to the group's healthy functioning (Gladding, 2012). These roles need to include individuals who are rule followers, but also those who are divergent thinkers. Some members must be collaborative and cooperative, while others must function with one foot in the individual realm. Some must be leaders while others must be comfortable following.

In essence, it is important to support diverse roles for group members in your classroom. This is essential for two reasons. First, it is advisable to avoid groupthink. Groupthink occurs when members lose their individual identity, when agreement with the group becomes more important than expressing valid but challenging positions. Groupthink is antithetical to good education. We want students to think for themselves, to come to their own conclusions, and certainly to advance the discussion through healthy and respectful disagreement. Groupthink prevents exactly these goals.

Moreover, there is a good deal of evidence to suggest that diverse groups make better decisions. James Surowiecki (2005) in his well-regarded book *The Wisdom of Crowds*, makes a compelling case that groups that possess healthy diversity come to better decisions than decisions arrived at by individuals, even when those individuals are experts. This can be very powerful for your classroom. As a result, your ability to tolerate differences yet build a healthy classroom community can set the stage for excellent decision making and learning along the way.

Small group work has become very popular in today's classrooms. The dynamics of the small group, or subgroup, are as important to pay attention to as the dynamics of the larger full classroom group (Gladding, 2012). Here again there are roles, and norms. Moreover, these groups are subgroups of the larger classroom group. As such, they are already influenced by, or in some cases contaminated by, the dynamics of the whole. The essential question to ask is "What have the students who make up these small groups learned about group functioning from the larger group?" If there is significant dysfunction at the more macro level, it is likely to be repeated here. The repetition may not be in the same form as in the larger group, but some dysfunction may be inevitable. Likewise, though, if the larger group functions in a healthy manner, it is more likely that smaller subset groups will as well.

Early in my teaching career I consulted with one of my mentors, now colleagues, about my teaching (Greenwood, 1995). He had observed my classroom and had several comments about the small group work my students were doing. In my naiveté I thought this work was going fine. I was oblivious to any problems as there were no obvious dysfunctions. He disagreed and pointed out several problems. In our discussion he went on to offer a suggestion which I had never before heard or considered. He theorized that many classroom small group activities did not work because students had not been taught how to work in the group. No time had been spent working on forming the group, developing norms, building cohesion, and planning productivity. Rather, groups were simply formed based on some rather arbitrary dimension, like seating arrangement, and expected to work. Why then, according to him, was it a surprise that they often did not? His message is a very valuable one. If, as most of us do, you plan to use group work as an educational tool, take time to prepare students to make the experience productive.

Classroom learning, however, at the end of the day is primarily an individual initiative with individual goals. The group can enhance this process, or detract from it. As a classroom teacher you can have an active part in the development of healthy group dynamics. At the very least, do not underestimate the power of the group as it impacts the learning community of your classroom.

Questions for Reflection and Discussion

1. Can you recall a time in your education when the class as a group either interfered with or advanced the learning process? What group dynamics were at play and how do you think they developed?
2. What implicit norms might students bring to your classroom that might conflict with your style of teaching or your goals for your classroom?
3. Why might it be a good exercise to have an outsider observe your classroom from the perspective of group dynamics?

CREATING A CULTURE OF INQUIRY

KEY TAKEAWAY

A good classroom embraces a culture where thinking deeply, questioning, and challenging are valued. Students in this classroom learn to value the inquiry process and will carry that skill with them regardless of the profession they choose.

I am certain that you want your students to become lifelong learners. You want them to have a hunger for knowledge that goes well beyond the classroom and well past their formal educational years. You want them to be curious, inquisitive, and eager to learn. For many students, though, it is less likely that this will occur without you leading them toward this goal. This process begins in the classroom as you build a culture of inquiry into your teaching and classroom management.

This culture of inquiry lays the foundation for a lifetime of learning. It teaches your students that the inquiry process is primary in the learning process. It shows students that being a good student requires an active mind that pushes traditions and limits, challenges theories, and probes deeply. It instills in students the belief that in order to learn deeply you must ask questions, wonder, probe, challenge, and even demand. Without this, learning becomes a passive process in which each student waits patiently to be "filled" with knowledge that is deemed important in a specific academic setting. Learning does not become a way of life. Rather it becomes something to endure until real life begins. Ironically of course, it is far less likely that real life will begin unless this culture of inquiry takes root.

Certainly there are specific content lessons to learn. Students need to know their multiplication tables, how to read, and basic science facts. But beyond such basics, real learning takes place in real life, not in the classroom. Giving students tools to have inquiring minds allows them the chance to benefit from life's lessons. Where and how those inquiries arise after formal schooling is complete is not important. It is simply important that your student is prepared for them when they occur.

For example, if a student chooses to become a physician, throughout her lifetime it is likely that our knowledge of diseases and treatments will grow dramatically. The specifics of what she learned in school will mean less and less. The skill of asking, probing, and even challenging will keep her in good stead. Perhaps less glamorously, suppose a student chooses to become a football coach. The same skills will likely guide his success as will guide our physician. His ability to challenge the traditional way of operating, to ask important questions, and to wonder deeply will be more likely to guide him as he develops a new offensive or defensive philosophy than any particular and narrow skill or content he memorized in school.

In order to instill this devotion to inquiry in your students you must do three things in your classrooms. You must allow it, you must model it, and you must demand it. Let's look at each component separately.

Students will not learn to inquire unless they are given permission to do so. This permission must be given both directly and indirectly. As a teacher you must tell students directly that you want them to be curious, to ask questions, to wonder aloud, and even to challenge you if they disagree. Students will not naturally do this. Rather, they will obey the social demand of the situation and acquiesce to the authority. You want them to do the opposite, but you must invite them to do so.

This will be a difficult invitation for them to accept. At first, they will not believe it to be genuine. They will doubt it and test it. This is understandable given that it will likely be new for them. So you must counteract these previous experiences and give them this permission often. Only over time will they begin to accept your invitation and take their first steps into the process.

You must also give them this message indirectly. When students do ask questions, probe, or even challenge, you must be careful about your response. You want to reinforce these behaviors and therefore you must reward them. You can reward them with attention and excitement. You can piggyback on their inquiry, involve other students, and celebrate this new skill. Other students will watch your reactions carefully. They will learn vicariously, and quickly, whether you are true to the word of your explicit message. They will see immediately if you are genuinely interested in them using this new skill, and they will either join the party or quickly abandon it.

The second component involves modeling this new approach. You must show students how to be curious. Stopping a lesson and asking "I wonder why this is?" shows students that you do not know all the answers and that you are interested in learning more. Following this question with time dedicated in class to looking something up or researching an unanswered question demonstrates that you really do value this endeavor and that you will show them how to do it. Using your smartboard or computer to search for answers to questions that have arisen in class or to examine whether others have wondered about these same things is a very valuable use of time. Students can then see how you think, how you search, how you wonder, and how you translate these inquiries into concrete actions.

Third, you must demand that your students engage in this new activity. It is likely that inviting them and modeling for them will not be enough. By demanding that they do this, again, you are showing your devotion to the process and your commitment to its importance. This demand must go far beyond the usual "Does anyone have any questions?" inquiry that is offered halfheartedly and responded to rarely. Rather, this demand calls for very specific and planned activities.

Three very concrete ways of demanding this new skill might be considered. First, students might be required to write down a question, any relevant question, at the end of each academic lesson. You might require them to do so on index cards or in their notebooks. The simple process of having to generate questions will be a good first step in this learning process. The questions at first will come slowly and it is likely that they will not be particularly deep or probing. Over time, however, your students will improve in this skill. Their questions will become more challenging and interesting.

As part of this process it might be wise to avoid the natural tendency to require your students to try to answer or research these questions. This additional burden will likely negatively impact question generation. Students will limit themselves only to questions which they can easily answer, directly contradicting the point of the inquiry lesson. Just let the questions be. Researching answers is another lesson altogether.

While students are doing this individually, demand that they do so as a group as well. Here you can use small or large groups, even the whole class together depending upon size. Hold a question brainstorm activity in which each group generates any question they would like about the subject matter at hand. No question is a bad question and no questions will need to be answered. All questions will then be presented to the class as a whole, along with additional questions you have generated. By sharing all of these questions with the group you will be showing students how little you all actually know about the content being studied and how the true value in the lesson will lie in future exploration. Moreover, you are giving them the subtle message that they might be interested in pursuing answers to these questions on their own if they want to advance their learning in any particular realm.

Finally, include the process of generating inquiries as part of your learning assessments. Give students an opportunity to demonstrate how they are improving on this very valuable skill. Give assignments in which they receive credit for generating interesting questions. Moreover, include the process of asking questions on their content exams. For example, conclude each exam with a question in which you ask students to generate two questions that they wish had been answered during these lessons. Allow them to receive credit for generating interesting and challenging questions. You might even choose one or two of the best of these and present answers to them when you return the test to your students. These special questions might qualify the student to receive extra credit as well.

It is unfortunately unlikely that students will become inquisitive lifelong learners without us giving them the tools to do so. The skills of inquiring, probing, and challenging are the essential tools. Use your classroom as the place where such inquiries are allowed, modeled, and then even demanded. These will be life skills that will benefit your students no matter what career path they eventually follow.

Questions for Reflection and Discussion

1. What educational, or life, experiences have helped you become a more inquisitive thinker? How have those experiences impacted your learning throughout life?
2. Do you think students can be taught to be more inquisitive, or is it simply a natural skill that one does or does not have? If it can be taught, what ideas do you have that might address this goal? Is it ever too late to learn this skill?
3. How might students of different ages be taught to become more inquisitive thinkers? What strategies might uniquely work in grade school, middle school, high school, or college?

PART IV

KNOWING YOUR STUDENTS

In this section you will focus on students. Getting to know your students as individuals and avoiding biased thinking are essential to becoming an excellent teacher.

CHAPTER 12

GETTING TO KNOW YOU...

KEY TAKEAWAY

Take time to get to know your students. Learn about their abilities, their interests, and their lives. Use that knowledge to creatively motivate, plan lessons, and help them to apply knowledge.

It is incredibly important to get to know your students. In fact, one could argue that a failure in this realm might block your ability to be a truly effective educator in the classroom. Getting to know your students is essential for four reasons.

First, one of the first jobs of a teacher at the start of a class or academic year is to get a clear understanding of her students' abilities and skills, as well as their deficits and struggles. I cannot think of any way a good teacher can tailor lessons to her students without securing this assessment. While it may be possible to get a cursory sense of their skill sets or a quick inventory of their content knowledge through an initial test or assessment, it is quite likely that this quick and dirty assessment will provide you with an underestimate of your students' true abilities.

In these quick assessments students will respond in kind to your generic approach; that is, they will respond with careful and safe responses based in modulated effort. They will not go all out; they will not try to prove themselves to you. This would be too risky as they will not know how the information might be used by you in the future. Thus, while a survey of their knowledge might give you a very general sense of their abilities and achievements, you should never mistake that performance as indicative of their true abilities.

Rather, a deep and valid assessment of your students' abilities and limitations will only be possible if you reach out to them and truly try to get to know them. They will respect this intentional initiative. They will be far more likely to reciprocate in kind, letting you in to see their strengths and their weaknesses at a far deeper level. It is only after you have seen these that you will be able to constructively and effectively plan lessons.

A second reason it is essential that you get to know your students involves how you will teach on a daily basis. An important part of teaching involves finding ways for students to relate to and connect with the material. Using examples that are relevant to their lives is an easy way to accomplish this. More importantly, it is an effective way. Students are far more likely to understand complex concepts and difficult points when a connection is made to something with which they are already familiar. Using this connection allows them to put the new learning into a familiar context. It allows them to use their brain power to focus on and analyze the new concept, without having to divide their attention between a new concept and a foreign example. Getting to know your students allows you to make connections to their world, to use examples and analogies which are already familiar to them, and thus allows them to devote their learning energy to the new material you want as their main focus.

Getting to know your students communicates that you see them as well-rounded people who live complex lives. They are not simply names or student numbers on your roll sheet. This is an immediate communication to them that you understand and appreciate that they have chosen to spend part of their time learning from you.

Moreover, you convey to them that you have an appreciation for the complexities of life—for the fact that at times life interferes with peoples' best original intentions. This is important to communicate since it will be better for both of you if they talk to you early if something outside of class is interfering with their learning. If they or a family member has been sick, if they are balancing work and school, if they are struggling with many difficult courses this semester, you as a teacher should want to know this early in the year. Knowing early allows both of you to do something constructive about learning problems, should they emerge. This is not at all to say that you will "go easy" on them; this is to say that you will respond as a fair and compassionate human being to their dilemma. Your response may not eventually be the response they would like to hear, or the response that makes things "easy" on them, but it will be a fair and compassionate response. You are far more likely to get the opportunity to work towards such a response if you get to know your students early in the process. Failing to do this will likely lead you and the student into the all too common situation in which problems are avoided until it is too late to productively address them.

Finally, motivation is important to the learning process. Part of your job as a teacher is to help motivate your students' learning. Again, this is hard to do without knowing your students. Students respond differently to various forms of motivation. Some need coaxing; some need prodding; some need encouragement; some need empowerment; and some need tough love. Each class will have some students who need each of these strategies in order to succeed. How will you know which student will respond positively to which strategies unless you have gotten to know them as individuals? If you only use tough love, either because it is the only tool in your box or because you misguidedly believe that all students need this, you will be successful with a small minority of students in your classroom. And that is not your job. Your job will always be to educate all your students.

Now that we've established its importance, how might you go about getting to know your students? Much of this is dependent upon the level you are teaching. Strategies will likely be rather different in a grade school, a middle school, a high school, or a college. The first strategy, however, cuts across all levels of education. Quite simply, at the start of the academic term, you must be a keen listener and observer. You must watch and listen to the students, particularly when they are not directly interacting with you. When they are directly interacting with you, you are likely to get well socialized and highly practiced interactions. These will not tell you who they really are; these will simply tell you how skilled they are at adapting to this educational culture. You need rawer data than this. You need to listen to their interactions with each other. What are they talking about? How do they interact? What words do they use? How do they express emotion? Whom are they connected to? Listening to and observing the students before class, during free time, and in the hallway will tell you who they really are.

In addition, scheduling learning activities that simultaneously allow you to get to know students and teach your content area can be a helpful part of an early term lesson plan. Worksheets, short presentations, and small group work that combine a personal component with content can work well. Creativity will be the key here, but almost every discipline should lend itself to some activity in which a truly creative teacher can combine personal introduction with discipline specific knowledge.

Getting to know your students as individuals is essential as well. Individual meetings are the best way to do so. In the younger grades, those individual meetings might involve the child's parents rather than the student him or herself. This is after all the purpose behind the commonly held parent-teacher conferences. Unfortunately, however, parent-teacher conferences are often held after the first quarter of an academic year. This is a wonderful time to meet if your purpose is only to review progress in the classroom. It is far too late to meet if your goal is to get to know your students. Some school districts have a "meet the teacher" night earlier in the semester. This is a very valuable opportunity to meet the parents of your students and learn a bit about them. Unfortunately many parents do not attend these evenings, and time is quite limited.

If you do have an opportunity to meet with parents early in the semester, asking them these three questions may be quite useful in getting to know their child: What are your child's strengths as a student and as a learner? What are your child's weaker areas as a learner? What strategies or approaches have helped your child learn in the past? If you have additional time beyond this, asking parents to describe their child's interests and interpersonal style can be helpful, but you will likely get this information as well through your own direct observations and planned activities during the first few weeks of the year.

At the more advanced levels of high school and college, individual, or if necessary, small group meetings near the start of an academic term are almost essential. These could be held in the classroom or in an office during office hours. These meetings should be planned and scheduled, and every student should be "encouraged" or required to participate. To create this welcoming environment, one of my colleagues has renamed her office hours as "student hours" (Hill, 2012). These meetings need not be long, often as brief as just a few minutes, and can be spread out over the first few weeks of the academic term. Asking one or two students to stay two minutes after class each day can even be effective.

Four questions should guide the content of these student meetings. It likely does not make sense to discuss how the student is doing thus far in the class or to review assessment of learning data at this time, as most likely little formal assessment has been completed. Instead, students should be asked: Why did you decide to take this class? What do you hope to learn in this class? How would you describe your style of learning? Is there anything that you have noticed that might need to change in order to improve your chances for learning in this class? By focusing on these four questions first, you are communicating to the student that you are most interested in his learning, that in fact you are as committed to his learning goals as he is.

Only after these questions are complete should you potentially ask more personal questions. Asking students very briefly about their hobbies, clubs, activities, and interests can allow you to connect with them at a different level. Care must be taken here, however, to respect the boundaries implied in the situation. Some students will readily share such personal details with you, while others will be far more reticent and reserved. This is their right and we as teachers must respect it. In no circumstances should you ask personal questions which might make the student at all uncomfortable. Conclude your individual meeting with a direct statement that it is your strong desire that they succeed in your classroom and that you are available to help them in that endeavor.

Invitations to talk again later in the term are important as well. Let students know exactly how and when they can get in contact with you. Explain your office hour, or student hour, and e-mail policies. Strongly encourage them to schedule follow up meetings with you later in the semester. And finally, use the knowledge you have gained about their learning styles to help tailor your course to the students sitting in your classroom this semester.

The final strategy useful to getting to know your students involves your activities outside the classroom. In essence I would recommend the following: Get involved. On a very informal level, simply be around. Walk around the lunchroom or cafeteria. Greet students in the hallways. Go to extra-curricular activities. Be a part of the school community. On a more formal level you might choose to become a faculty leader or sponsor for an activity, club, or sport. Moderate the student council, coach the cross country team, begin a French club. It does not have to be a formal role, but certainly a formal role can have increased payoffs.

In essence, you become a better teacher when you know your students. Moreover, your job will often be far more fulfilling when you add this personal touch to your educational expertise.

Questions for Reflection and Discussion

1. What do you think of the strategy of getting to know your students by talking with their former teachers? What might be the positive and negative aspects to this strategy?
2. What boundaries must you keep in mind when getting to know your students?
3. What activities or exercises from your particular discipline might be adapted to include a "getting to know you" component?

APPRECIATING LEARNING STYLES

KEY TAKEAWAY

The topic of learning styles is a controversial one. Scientists debate whether different learning styles exist and how they impact learning. One differentiation that seems to be helpful is the distinction between reflective and active learners. As a teacher you must construct lessons and assessments for all types of learners.

Discussions of learning styles have been popular for many decades now. Encouraging educators to teach to different learning styles has almost become cliché. This is both a good and a bad thing. On the positive side of the ledger, the commonality of this discussion suggests that almost all teachers are now aware of the concept and are trained to vary their educational methods. On the negative side, however, it may be that we have stopped examining the issue critically and thus stopped innovating in its application.

As such, a short discussion of the topic of learning styles is certainly germane to this book. The reader should be aware that this discussion cannot hope to cover the myriad of applications of this concept proposed over the past forty years. Rather this discussion is offered in hopes of directing, or redirecting, the teacher's attention to this important, if still somewhat controversial, issue.

Although numerous books and articles have been published on the topic of learning styles over the past forty plus years, not everyone endorses the concept as either important or scientifically sound. Several writers over the years have suggested that the concept lacks scientific rigor and that there have been few, if any, studies documenting its validity and/or usefulness as a scientific construct. Perhaps most interestingly, the American Psychological Society (APS) asked a group of renowned cognitive scientists to examine the literature on this issue and offer a scientific analysis. In essence, this report argued that few if any valid empirical studies had been completed on this concept and that such studies really should be done before more work on implementation and application occurs (Pashler, McDaniel, Rohrer, & Bjork, 2008). Thus, educators today should understand that although we discuss the concept of learning styles as if it is non-controversial and universally accepted, it is not. As such, we must be careful about its application.

A traditional discussion of learning styles often contrasts the visual learner with the auditory learner. The visual learner is one who learns best by using materials that can be processed visually, such as pictures, films, charts, diagrams, and the like. In contrast, the auditory learner prefers to process the world through her sense of hearing. She learns best when concepts are explained orally, often through lecture and discussion. All of us are capable of learning through both the auditory and the visual channels. Some of us, however, appear to learn better through one channel over the other. It becomes quite obvious that a teacher must understand whether her students are likely to learn auditorially or visually in order to maximize each student's learning.

More recently the concept of experiential learning has become popular. Sometimes in the literature this is labeled as kinesthetic learning. Whether labeled as experiential or kinesthetic, the point is the same. Students who learn well using this style are those who do something actively with the material. They literally learn best when they physically interact with the material, perhaps through a field trip, a dramatization, a role play, a laboratory, or some other activity.

Because of the complexity of the topic of learning styles and the rather unique vocabulary that has emerged in the scientific literature devoted to this topic, many educators leave school with only this rudimentary understanding of learning styles. That is, learners are either visual or auditory, and maybe experiential. There is little discussion of the topic beyond this. If in fact this concept proves to be a valid scientific construct, it is likely that it will prove to be far more complex than this model, and that the interaction between learning style and actual learning will be quite complex indeed. Thus, while it is good that teachers today at least consider these three styles, they must also realize that this simple division may not do justice to the concept.

For example, Felder and Soloman (2012), as well as other writers over the years, have differentiated between what they call active learners vs. reflective learners. This is an interesting differentiation that may be more relevant than the division discussed above. Active learners are those who learn best when they must do something "active" to the to-be-learned material. These are students who learn best when they have to explain it to others, quiz each other, or teach a lesson based on this content. In contrast, reflective learners learn best when they ponder over what they are internalizing. These students do best when they are left alone to think, untangle, and apply the lessons. In fact, prompted interaction with others might actually interfere with their learning. Quite obviously, these are two very different types of learners, and educational exercises must be carefully planned for each group.

In light of the fact then that we could never cover the totality of the literature on learning styles in a brief text such as this, allow me to offer five simple guidelines for your consideration. Paying attention to each of these should at least provide you with a foundation upon which further refined applications can be built. While the research on learning styles will no doubt advance over the next many years, keeping these five guidelines in mind will allow you to use new developments to benefit your students.

1. Do not rely too heavily on your own learning style as a guide for your lesson planning. You no doubt know by now that you are a verbal or auditory learner. Perhaps you are active or maybe more reflective. Be careful with that knowledge. You must move outside your comfort zone as you lesson plan. Your lesson plans must be inclusive of students who learn quite differently than you.
2. Each academic term try to assess the preferred learning styles of your students. This assessment can be both formal and informal. Asking students to complete on-line learning styles questionnaires is easy and efficient if your students are old enough. There are many offered free of charge on-line and students could then share their results with you. Informal assessment, primarily through careful observation, will be important as well. This will be particularly important when your students are too young to have metacognitive awareness of their own learning. By using a variety of teaching techniques and assignments during the first part of a term, an observant teacher should have a good sense of her students' general learning styles.
3. Use the knowledge from your formal and informal learning styles assessments to guide your lesson planning. Make sure to include important lesson strategies that appeal to each type of learning style. That is, give students a fair opportunity to learn using the channel that works best for them. In addition, remember that we all learn at least in part through all channels. Presenting important lessons using multiple learning channels then will aid all students, not just those with a particular learning style.
4. Consider some targeted teaching and assignments. Group work is a part of most classrooms now, at almost every level of education. Dividing your class into groups based on learning style, rather than on other common factors, might be incredibly productive. Matching the group task with that learning style then might be a quite efficient use of time. For example, asking a group of experiential learners to develop a short script or role play relating to the topic, while a more visually oriented group developed a chart or even artistic depiction of the concept, while still a third group engaged in a structured discussion might be a valuable use of limited time.
5. Finally, do not forget that multimodal teaching must be followed up with multimodal assessment. While this topic is covered more extensively in Chapter 20, it should be mentioned briefly here. Students should have the opportunity to demonstrate their learning using different formats, just as they have learned through various modalities. To teach to different styles, and then not assess through those same styles is inconsistent and of questionable validity. For example, visual students should not just be taught visually; their learning should be assessed through a visually based assignment. The same of course applies to students of all different learning styles.

Granted, the literature on learning styles is overwhelming and it is difficult for an educator to stay current on the topic. The issue is complex, and we do not yet have a good understanding of its complexity. Moreover, it remains valid that the concept, and our understanding and application of it, remain scientifically unproven. Still, common sense tells us that staying open to the concept and its application will likely allow you to reach more of your students.

Questions for Reflection and Discussion

1. Do you have a good sense of your own learning style? How would you describe it? When did you become aware of it, and how? Has that knowledge benefitted you in any way?
2. Reflecting back on your own educational history, how would you describe how various learning styles were addressed in the classroom?
3. Why do you think the topic of learning styles is so controversial? What is it about the concept, or its application, that seems to energize discussions of the topic?

UNDERSTANDING STANDARDIZED TESTS

<table>
<tr><td>

KEY TAKEAWAY

Aptitude tests measure potential for learning. Achievement tests measure what was learned. Be careful not to mix the two purposes. Be careful not to let tests of questionable validity prejudice your assessment of your students' learning.
</td></tr>
</table>

You will often be surprised by what your students can and will learn, particularly when they are taught well. They will be able to stretch to heights that could not have been predicted. In point of fact, you, and they, will often have been told that these heights were unattainable. Do not believe this.

The field of psychology differentiates between achievement tests and aptitude tests. Achievement tests are designed to measure how much students have learned. For example, a math test that asks third grade students to answer multiplication questions after learning multiplication tables is an achievement test. It answers the question "Did my student learn the lesson?" Aptitude tests are much different. The SAT (Scholastic Aptitude Test), and perhaps to a slightly lesser extent, the ACT (American College Test) are purportedly primarily aptitude tests. They are designed to measure potential rather than previous learning. Students take both types of tests during their academic careers. It is important though to keep these two tests separate in your mind.

One area which holds students back and tempers our expectations for student learning is the results of standardized aptitude tests. Since standardized aptitude tests purport to predict a student's learning potential, they are potentially dangerous instruments. If they are not valid and reliable they may do more damage than good. Many writers have questioned their validity, especially around the issue of culture (Jaschik, 2010; Freedle, 2003; Santelices & Wilson, 2010). Others have argued though that these tests are not particularly valid for any culture, and certainly not valid in predicting anything beyond school success (Fairtest, 2007). It could even be argued though that they do in fact predict students' learning potential, when that student is provided with mediocre teaching. That is, they may be far less predictive when we teach well.

Thus a first caution involves your expectations as a teacher. In an earlier essay I wrote about being "greedy" as a teacher. Unfortunately, sometimes our societal obsession with testing interferes with our ability to become greedy. When your "greed" is tempered by your students' aptitude limitations as measured by aptitude testing, a warning flag should be raised. You are entering into a very dangerous zone. The last thing you want is to have your limited expectations become the ceiling for your students' learning. Students will find their own ceiling. It is not your job to try to predict it before they have a chance to test it.

A second caution involves being careful as you construct your assessments of student learning. Let's look at this logically. Assessment of student learning should be exactly that—evaluation of prior learning. It should not be a measure of aptitude, intelligence, potential, or something other than achievement. Therefore, you have to carefully construct your measures of assessment. While an entire essay has been devoted to this complex topic of assessment, allow me to reinforce an idea here -- assessment of learning needs to be a measurement of achievement rather than aptitude.

This brings us to the complicated issue of the role of standardized testing in education. Standardized testing has become a societal obsession. Every year millions of children are subjected to purported assessments of learning that appear to be some hybrid of achievement and aptitude. It is unclear what it is that is being measured, yet it is measured over and over again. Moreover, important educational and career decisions are being based on the outcomes of these tests. Expectations of future learning are communicated to students, as well as to parents and teachers, based on these results, and sometimes teachers are even rewarded or punished based on these results. In addition, it has become big business. Millions, if not billions of dollars are now spent on "prep" classes for the SAT and ACT tests. All of this even though we are quite unsure what it is we are measuring.

And that is the gist of the problem. If we all agreed that a third grader should know these 100 things and then we tested the third grader for knowledge of these 100 things, the process would be transparent and fair. But we neither agree on the 100 things nor do we agree how to assess learning of these 100 things. Instead, we construct tests that are not true achievement measures. Rather, they are hybrid achievement/aptitude measures. They mix the idea of previous learning with potential. We are left with a mess of results that we really cannot understand. Yet we purport to understand it quite clearly and make important life decisions based upon these interpretations.

Moreover, we then repeat the same mistakes in our own classrooms. We construct tests that are similar achievement/aptitude hybrids. We feel good when our best students do best on the exams and we are not surprised when our lower aptitude students struggle. But should we really feel good? If all we have done is give an aptitude loaded test to students, how could we be surprised when the students who previously were identified as high aptitude again score highest? How could they not? And what have we learned about what our students have learned and how well we have taught the lessons? Very little.

Even on their own, pure aptitude tests are likely deserving of question and challenge. These tests are designed to predict success in future education. IQ tests predict school learning; the ACT and SAT are designed to predict success in college; and the GRE predicts academic success in graduate school. But that is all these predict—academic success. Even the test constructors themselves do not argue that the predictive ability of these tests goes beyond the classroom. Success in the real world appears to be at least in part the byproduct of important personality variables like motivation and persistence rather than simply due to pure aptitude (Heckman, 2010; Tough, 2011). Does this not beg the question then of why we are measuring aptitude? If we are just predicting success in school, but not later life, this seems like a very meager purpose.

In essence, then we are left with two significant testing problems. First, too often achievement tests are "contaminated" by aptitude questions. This occurs both within individual classrooms as well as on grander scales. Second, aptitude test results are of questionable, or at least limited, use. Since we know that many of these tests have significant cultural validity questions, that they only seem to predict school learning well, and that some people appear to be poor test takers rather than poor learners, we are left with many questions about the validity of these tests.

All of this should engender caution in your use of standardized tests. A good achievement test is incredibly valuable. It tells you what your students have learned. In so doing it tells you where you have succeeded and failed as a teacher. But this test must truly be a measure of achievement. A good aptitude test has a legitimate place too. When you are truly trying to predict future school learning, such tests can be very accurate. You simply cannot delude yourself into thinking that these tests go beyond these uses.

Questions for Reflection and Discussion

1. What are your views of standardized educational testing? How have your own personal experiences with such testing impacted your views?
2. What are the pros and cons of relying on standardized educational testing in our schools? Do you think we have gone too far, or perhaps not far enough, in its use?
3. How might you defend against the common pitfall of designing methods of assessment which inadvertently measure aptitude rather than achievement?

AVOIDING GENDER, AND OTHER, BIASES
IN THE CLASSROOM

KEY TAKEAWAY

There is research evidence that many classrooms harbor, no doubt unintentionally, a great deal of bias. Be vigilant for its obvious and subtle expression in your classroom.

It is more than a bit disturbing that a major clothing retailer recently advertised a tee shirt for girls that had this message on the front: "I'm too pretty to do math." My guess is the shirt sold well.

Recently the American Association of University Women (AAUW) put forth a major paper addressing gender bias in education (Hill, Corbett, and St. Rose, 2010). This report, entitled "Why So Few?" attempted to document and provide recommendations to improve the fact that few girls were pursuing the science, technology, engineering, and mathematics (i.e. the so called STEM fields) disciplines in college and in their career choices. This report discusses the biases, both societal and unconscious, which seem to play a large role in this problem. In addition, the report offers several concrete suggestions to try to address these biases early in a girl's educational career.

Not too long ago, Myra and David Sadker authored an important work on the issue of gender bias in education (Sadker and Sadker, 1995). This book entitled *Failing at Fairness: How Our Schools Cheat Girls* discussed both the subtle and obvious ways in which gender biases contaminate our work as educators, even lurking silently in the day to day workings of our classrooms. One of the more important essays contained in this volume was entitled "Hidden Lessons." Here the Sadkers explain the development of a careful class observation system they developed to aid their research. After much training and development, the researchers collected thousands of direct classroom observations. These observations revealed that there was significant gender bias at play in classrooms and that the gender bias was often subtle, but profound. In essence, teachers tended to interact with male students more, prompting them with better questions and offering them superior feedback to their female peers. Interestingly, Dateline NBC completed a segment describing the Sadkers' research and work. When that segment was under production, the producers (two females) had great difficulty finding the bias in the teacher demonstration tapes.

It was not until the producers were educated about such subtle bias that the examples became obvious. Clearly, the socialization process over the years had been effective.

The overarching point is a simple one. The classroom is a place where societal biases can easily be continued and acted out, even when it is your best intention not to do so. Being careful is not enough. Carefully monitoring yourself for these inevitable biases may not even be enough. You may need to ask others to evaluate your efforts and effectiveness in this realm.

The most problematic position one could take on this issue would be that he or she is immune to such biases. The human condition likely makes that an impossibility. After all, we naturally categorize, summarize, judge, and evaluate. Our brains work towards efficiency, which often is reductive in its effects. When we reduce, when we simplify, we lose subtle differences. We gloss over individual uniqueness and overgeneralize in our categorization. As such, biases are simply inevitable.

A more productive approach is to acknowledge that we, like everyone else, engage in this type of reductionistic thinking. And as a result, we carry biases into our work. Because your workplace is the classroom, this has profound effects on society and society's future. If you acknowledge that you too succumb to this natural limitation, you can begin to explore where you fall victim and how it impacts your work. Beginning this self-evaluation with a curious and inquisitive mind, rather than a defensive one, will increase the likelihood that you will be able to accurately identify your biases, and do something to minimize them.

Of course these biases go well beyond gender. We have our biases about many aspects of culture. Ethnic biases, disability biases, age biases, and physical biases are common, perhaps even universal. It is when these biases begin to interfere with offering an equal and fair education to all of our students that we must worry.

An interesting exercise to explore one's own biases can be completed online. Psychologists from Harvard University have developed a way for us to privately assess our own biases. A test entitled the Implicit Associations Test (IAT) seeks to evaluate our biases, even those of which we may not be consciously aware (Project Implicit, 2011). The test examines potential biases we might hold in such areas as race, age, religion, physical features, skin tone, gender, sexuality, and disabilities. It involves providing quick timed reactions to words and images presented online. Reaction times are then analyzed and interpreted as reflective of our conscious and unconscious attitudes. The results can be challenging, even disturbing. We often have to face the idea that some of our biases lie in surprising areas.

An examination or evaluation, whether it be the IAT or some other assessment instrument, should be the beginning, rather than the end of our exploration. It is not enough to simply know your biases, although this is certainly a very good first step. Rather, now is the time to make sure those biases are not interfering with your students' education. Here is where you must become a vigilant planner. Consciously planning lessons that do not have hidden biases and managing your classroom in ways that do not communicate even subtly biased messages are essential steps in the process.

Because our biases often effectively hide themselves from us, this is usually the place where external aid can be beneficial. Asking others to review your lesson plans and to observe your teaching with the explicit instruction to point out any potential biases can be quite helpful. Quite literally, a fresh pair of eyes here is usually essential to see these biases. Even this though may not be enough. Like the Dateline producers who struggled to identify the bias in the videotapes until directly trained to do so, many of the biases are deeply interwoven into our culture. As such, they are part and parcel of who we are and we have been extensively socialized not to see them, in both ourselves and others. It will likely take significant effort and expense to counteract that cultural trend, but one of your students may thank you some day for encouraging her more than anyone else did throughout her education.

Questions for Discussion and Reflection

1. Do you think we all have at least one, if not many more, hidden biases? Where did they come from? What is society's role in this process? What is biology's role?
2. Can you identify one area where you might have a hidden bias, or one area which at least demands some reflection and examination? What leads you to suspect that you may have a hidden bias in this area? What might you do about it to limit its impact?
3. Consider taking the IAT online. If you do choose to do so, carefully and critically evaluate both the process and your results. What did you think of the test? Do you think it is valid? What are its weaknesses? What did you think of your results?

DEALING WITH DISABILITIES

KEY TAKEAWAY

Working with students with disabilities should challenge and excite you. Working to find appropriate accommodations and modifications will allow you to creatively lesson plan and meet your goal of helping all of your students learn.

Your job is to teach all of your students. Some learn readily and seemingly effortlessly. For these students, simple exposure to the material is often enough. Others, however, struggle to learn. One subset of learners whom we are charged with educating are students with disabilities. These students often struggle in the classroom. While teaching students with disabilities can at times challenge our creative teaching skills, it is an endeavor worth undertaking. Here is where you really earn your stripes.

A disability is "a physical or mental impairment that substantially limits one or more of the major life activities of such individual" (Americans with Disabilities Act of 1990; Public L. 101–336, 2, 104 Stat. 328(1991)). In this case, the major life activity would be learning, specifically in school. Disabilities which often impact learning vary widely, but some of the most common ones are learning disabilities, autism, psychiatric conditions, and sensory impairments. Individuals with disabilities have special rights and protections by law.

Disabilities can interfere with learning in the classroom. When they do, students are insured certain legal rights and protections. Young students at the elementary and high school level are granted these rights through the Individuals with Disabilities Educational Act, with its most recent iteration having been passed into law in 2004 (United States Code, 20 U.S.C.1401 {30}). This act is usually referred to as IDEA 2004. This law specifies the process by which a child can be granted special education status, their subsequent rights, and the resultant responsibilities of those educating this child. It is a lengthy law with very specific requirements. Teachers working at these educational levels, even those not teaching in a special education classroom, need to be well versed in IDEA 2004.

IDEA 2004 does not cover college education. Individuals with disabilities still have protected rights at this level though. These protections are rooted in the Americans with Disabilities Act, more specifically Section 504 of this act (Americans with Disabilities Act of 1990; Public L. 101–336, 2, 104 Stat. 328(1991)). These protections are not as specific as those delineated under IDEA 2004, but they constitute the legal foundation for disability services at the college and post-collegiate level. All college teachers should be familiar with this law.

How do these laws impact teaching in the classroom? While most of the legal issues related to these laws will not directly involve the classroom teacher, the process of providing education to special education students will of course remain your responsibility. This will be most clearly seen in the modifications and accommodations offered to your students to help them improve their learning. As a classroom teacher you will be responsible for implementing, monitoring, and evaluating these modifications and accommodations, as well as proposing ones which will further improve the learning process.

It is important to understand the philosophy behind modifications and accommodations. Simply put, modifications and accommodations are designed to "level the playing field" in the classroom. That is what individuals with disabilities have the legal right to—a level playing field. If you begin to think about disabilities in these terms, the modification process begins to make more sense. It would not make sense to insist that a visually impaired child read from a standard text book. Using Braille or audio books levels the playing field by allowing a visually impaired student access to the same content as his peers. A child with a neurologically based memory disorder cannot remember his multiplication tables. Allowing him to use a calculator or multiplication card gives him access to learning higher level mathematical ideas. Modifications and accommodations remove barriers, or allow students to move around barriers, in order to insure further learning opportunities. It is really that simple.

Just as no two non-disabled students are identical in their learning approach, neither are any two disabled students. Each student's disability impacts his processing of information in a way as unique as his individual brain. As such, modifications are unique to each disability and each individual. Standard accommodations are almost by definition inadequate. Despite this, often standard accommodations are implemented, unfortunately depriving the creative classroom teacher of a golden teaching opportunity.

Having the opportunity to educate a student with a disability is a wonderful opportunity for any classroom teacher. Creatively finding a way to teach material which otherwise might be out of the reach of a student should present an exciting challenge for any teacher. A first step in that process is to own the idea of modifications and accommodations. Modifications and accommodations are seen too often as external burdens, mandated by administrators or non-teaching school personnel. Creating effective accommodations and modifications though should be seen as an opportunity to break away from that mindset. If you as a teacher dedicate yourself to creatively intervening with every student, to working hard to reach every student, to devoting your energy to creative teaching techniques, then modifications can be seen as an exciting challenge rather than a depleting burden.

Too often odd philosophical objections are raised in response to being asked to make curricular or programmatic accommodations and modifications. It is common to hear such objections as "It is not fair to the other students in the room" and "If I do this for one student I have to do it for everyone." These are completely illogical statements, turning the issue of fairness on its head. The fairness principle here is only relevant as it involves a student with a disability. The non-disabled student does not need an accommodation to learn. Providing one to the non-disabled students "out of fairness" is nonsensical, and perhaps bad teaching. Each student should get what he or she needs to learn. Every student should not get what another student needs to learn. There is simply no logic in that.

Other times objections come on more practical grounds. It is not uncommon to hear complaints such as "Why should I have to create these modifications?" or "All of these accommodations take me too much time." These types of comments should raise immediate concerns. Instead of seeing these situations as opportunities, they are being perceived as burdens. This response usually occurs when teachers are already overburdened for other reasons. Obviously relieving that overburdening by not developing appropriate learning lessons is not a solution that benefits anyone. Instead, these comments are an alert that something in the educational system is not working, that the teacher is feeling overwhelmed. It is that issue that should be addressed, rather than punishing the child with the disability.

Once in a while this objection is voiced: "I don't really believe in all of these disabilities." I am sorry to say that really there is only one response to such an uninformed comment. A teacher with this perspective has not been well educated on the sciences of cognition, learning, and brain processing. It is not a debatable issue as to whether specific cognitive disabilities exist and interfere with learning. The science is overwhelming and those with doubt should be offered a re-education in this area.

A good teacher is always monitoring what is working and not working for each student in her classroom. This is exactly what is needed in planning, developing, and implementing modifications. Trying new techniques, doing whatever is necessary to help a child learn, finding the key to each child's mind—this is what teaching is all about. Just as in teaching non-disabled students, the focus of your efforts should be on ensuring learning. Your focus as a teacher should be on neither legal issues nor philosophical arguments related to teaching students with disabilities. Your laser focus must remain on teaching so that all of your students can learn.

Questions for Reflection and Discussion

1. Do you have any preconceived ideas about disabilities, either positive or negative? How do you think you developed these? How might they impact your work with disabled students in your classroom? What steps might you take to insure that students with disabilities receive their rights and protections in your classroom?

2. Why do you think some teachers complain about having to provide modifications and accommodations to students with disabilities? Is it just a time issue or is there more to it?
3. Why do you think we tend to rely heavily on a set of standard accommodations for children with many disabilities, rather than modifications and accommodations tailored to each unique child?

PART V

TEACHING

In this section you will focus on what you can do in the classroom to make sure that your students are learning.

PLANNING LESSONS: KNOW YOUR TOP THREE

KEY TAKEAWAY

Your students will remember little of the content you teach. Plan what you want them to remember by identifying, emphasizing, and repeating the most important three points from each lesson, each week, and each academic term.

Many students retain very little from the lessons we teach them. We bemoan this fact on a regular basis, and somehow seem surprised by its reoccurrence just as often. The reality is that most of what we teach our students will not be remembered by them. While this thought is discouraging, and if we let it grow, even demoralizing, it remains reality. Instead of succumbing to this defeat, however, perhaps a well-planned approach to this dilemma is warranted.

This issue may be somewhat less of a problem if you teach young children. Here kids are learning foundational skills from you. Reading and arithmetic are skills that stay with you throughout life. But as children get older and take more content oriented courses, the focus is on learning facts rather than skills. Here is where we as teachers often have unrealistic expectations and must face the inevitable disappointment that follows. Students in Chemistry, US History, English Literature, Social Studies, General Psychology and other discipline specific courses simply will not retain most of what we teach to them.

One way to manage this problem is to focus on "your top three." This idea is quite simple and can be applied in almost any classroom. The "top three" here refers to the three most important things you want students to learn in any particular time period. Since it is highly unlikely that students will retain more than three important pieces of information, a focus on the top three can be quite effective.

This method works best if it is shared with students. Telling students that each class will focus on three key ideas helps structure the lesson for both you and them. Focusing a lesson around three important points helps prioritize the learning process for the student. These three ideas then become the focus of the class. As you introduce each, it is labeled as one of the key ideas for the day. As you conclude discussion of that idea or explanation of that concept, you can reiterate its importance by labeling it as one of the "top three" for the day. As you conclude class you can review each of the three, leaving students with a clear message as to what is important, what you expect them to understand, and what you hope they will remember. The next class period can be started with a quick review of the top three from the day before, reorienting students to both the content of the lesson as well as your teaching strategy.

The notion of a "top three" becomes more powerful when it is applied across time frames. While the idea of each lesson having a "top three" is powerful, there is no need to restrict the idea to a single class period. Each week, month, and academic term can have its own "top three." In this model then, each week is begun with a review of the previous week's top three. This builds a bridge from the previous week's content to the current week's content. Moreover, each academic term can be focused on its own "top three." These three key ideas would likely flow from the weekly "top threes" you already emphasized. This provides a powerful organizing structure for student learning.

One key to the success of this strategy is that you make the "top three" very clear to the student. You do not rely on students to divine the top three on their own. You explicitly label the top three concepts, ideas, or skills as they are taught in class. You label them as one of the three most important things to retain from that day's lesson. You direct students to focus their attention on these top three points, as you teach them in class, as they read their text book, and as they complete assignments. In addition, it can be quite helpful to reinforce their importance by emphasizing the three, and only these three, in homework assignments. This allows students to carry the top three outside of the classroom. Moreover, this emphasis can structure and focus your student interactions. In essence, making the top three explicit is a necessary part of this process.

This strategy will require a good deal of planning on your part. First, you must be very clear in your mind as to what those top three ideas or concepts entail. If you are unclear, students will choose their own "top three." This is not likely to be a successful experience as it is unlikely they will choose the most important "top three."

In addition, daily, weekly, and term lessons need to be planned so as to emphasize these "top three." This is not an easy task the first time around, but it will be worth the investment. If you teach the same class in subsequent terms, however, you will have already clearly established your "top three" in your mind. More of your planning time can then be spent on creative ways to emphasize these three points, rather than spending time fretting that you have not covered enough material.

One might object to this method with the notion that students should figure out the "top three" on their own, that this search is part of the learning process. While there is some truth to this, this criticism probably only is fair in very advanced courses or levels of education. Before that too many students are unable to do this sophisticated metacognitive task. Instead, what happens is that all concepts, ideas, and skills are evaluated as equally important. The sheer number of things to learn is thus overwhelming, and as a result, little long term learning is accomplished. Moreover, what of the students, and there would be many, who never figure out the correct "top three?" Should they be deprived of learning important skills and concepts because of this metacognitive failure? Such seems a steep punishment for a simple developmental failure.

This new strategy will likely take some adjustment on your part. You will initially worry, and probably feel guilty, that you are not covering enough material, that your students will not do well on their standardized tests, and that someone will criticize your teaching. In fact, however, the opposite will likely occur. Students will retain the important material, other teachers will comment that your students are very well prepared when they reach their class at the next level, your students will deeply understand the core concepts and be more likely to demonstrate that knowledge on standardized tests, and in the end, you will be praised for being an effective teacher.

Questions for Reflection and Discussion

1. Honestly reflect on your own learning throughout your schooling. How much information did you retain from class to class? How much information made it from one semester to the next? How often did you simply cram information for an exam, purging it before learning new material? How might this teaching strategy of focusing on the top three ideas have helped you avoid this problem and made your learning more effective?
2. Think about a time in which you took a class and felt overwhelmed by the sheer volume of material. What strategies did you use to reduce that material down to a manageable amount? How did you perform in that class? Would it have aided you if the teacher had explicitly focused on a "top three?"
3. Why do you think it is difficult for experts in their field to reduce information to three essential points?

TEACHING TO MASTERY

KEY TAKEAWAY

Simply exposing students to new ideas and experiences is not enough for true learning to occur. Exposure is not teaching. Teaching to mastery is the appropriate educational goal and one that gives all students, not just the ones with naturally high aptitudes, the opportunity to shine.

I worry that somewhere along the educational path we made a wrong turn. We took a path that endorsed the idea that our students need exposure to a wide breadth of material. This path was certainly alluring at the juncture. It is easy to see why we took the path. This path offered our students the opportunity to be exposed to all sorts of new ideas and experiences. Who would not want their students to be exposed to creative and stimulating ideas?

Unfortunately, danger also lurked, quietly and unobtrusively on this path. As we progressed further on the path, using more and more of our time and resources, we neglected our essence. We forgot that students could not really benefit from these diverse experiences unless they had already mastered the essentials. As such, we ended up building a house with no foundation. We often exposed them to much but we asked them to master very little. In essence, it was fool's gold.

In other words, we have often utilized an exposure model over a mastery model. We rarely insist that students master material before we move on either to new material or applications. We succumb to the pressure to move on, to make sure that we "cover" everything. What if we logically examined and evaluated the premise that underlies this educational emphasis, that students learn best through exposure? This may give us insight into how and where we have failed in our attempts to reconnoiter the learning path.

The first logical challenge is obvious, at least in retrospect. Exposing students to ideas is not the same as teaching them. Exposing students to ideas may be a way of enticing them to learn, but it is not equivalent to teaching. Teaching involves so much more. Teaching involves motivating, explaining, relating, applying, examining, reviewing, assessing, and connecting. These processes of course take time, sometimes significant amounts of it. Exposure does not. Exposure is quick and then you move on. So much more can be "covered" with exposure; much less is "covered" with true teaching. When the demand is to finish the book or make sure you complete the entire mandated curriculum, you are only left with one option—exposure.

Second, we are often tricked into thinking that exposure actually does work, that it is sufficient for learning. This mistaken conclusion occurs because exposure does in fact work for some students. Students who are self-motivated with very high aptitudes do often learn simply through exposure. Ideas are presented to these students and with very little effort the concepts are learned. These students are very lucky. Their natural aptitudes allow for them to profit from this method. And when they do we mistakenly conclude that everyone should be able to do so as well. In fact, in retrospect, this conclusion is patently false. Students who are not as independently self-motivated or who are not naturally quite as able simply need more in order to understand, integrate, and apply knowledge.

Think about an area in which you are not well versed. It can be any area. Perhaps you know nothing about building furniture or wiring a circuit. How competent would you feel in this endeavor if you simply watched an online video touching on the topic? Moreover, how would you feel if you could only watch the video once or twice? More importantly, how well will you have learned how to build furniture or wire a circuit? I would dare say that I would not want to sit in that chair or turn on that switch. Would you?

This is what we have asked our students to do. Quite often they are merely exposed to a topic and expected to demonstrate mastery of it. Certainly some students can do this. Just as someone naturally gifted in woodworking might be able to make a good chair after watching the aforementioned video, some students learn the latest scientific theory or mathematical challenge through exposure. Most of us though do not.

A third flaw is that this problem is then exacerbated going forward. Following the exposure, students are expected to use their new knowledge. They must apply it, build on it, and use it as the foundation for the learning of the next concept. But remember, it really has not been learned. As a result, all of the learning based on this faulty foundation is vulnerable as well. This new learning will be no better than the foundation upon which it was built.

So why do we do this? One primary reason is that mastery is boring while exposure is exciting. Students naturally want to hear something new every day. Moreover, it is more exciting for us as well. Examining a new idea or a new application may be far more exciting to everyone in the classroom, students and teachers alike.

Repeating the same lesson until learned can lead to drudgery, but it does not have to. This is where you must earn your money as a teacher. Here is where creativity comes into play. Mastery does not mean repetition of the same methods. Teaching to mastery means finding many different roads to the same end so that the lesson can be learned deeply by all.

Assessment of learning is impacted here as well. Assessment of learning becomes much more valid and more meaningful if we teach for mastery. If we use exposure methods we should not, maybe even could not, be surprised by our assessment results. Those students with the highest natural aptitude and motivation, those who performed best on the standardized aptitude tests, will learn the best. Others will likely learn only in line with their natural abilities. And therein lies the problem. If everyone performs exactly as his or her aptitude would predict, what have we added to the equation? What "teaching" has really occurred?

Most of us who have gone into education believe that there is more to the process than simply exposing our natural learners to ideas and then measuring their understanding. You have likely gone into teaching with some belief that you can help all students, that you can push beyond natural limits to help students learn more than either they or others might have predicted. Therein lies the joy of teaching. In allowing for a curriculum based in exposure over mastery we have deprived ourselves of this joyous opportunity and likely stolen a future from too many a student.

In some ways one might argue that in relying on exposure methods we are preventing our students from overachieving. Overachieving used to be, and maybe still is, a valued outcome. Many individuals proudly proclaim to be overachievers, and they are often celebrated for this. The message is clear—they have, through hard work achieved beyond what others thought they could do. One could even argue that this is one of the core essences of our culture, of the "American" way. Overachieving was not a bad thing; it was something to aspire to. Exposure strategies effectively limit, if not prevent, overachieving. Again, the most able achieve best, and everyone else achieves only in line with their "natural" abilities.

Teaching to mastery gives all students an opportunity to shine. It does not penalize those who come to things quickly and effortlessly. These advanced students can move on more quickly to the next concept or application. Nor does it penalize those who learn at a slower pace. Most importantly, it builds our pool of successful students and expands their opportunities, and their future successes.

This approach makes sense from both an individual and societal perspective. Individually, more students learn and succeed. More broadly, more students are able to contribute effectively, even grandly, to society. Fewer students are left poorly educated, with deficient basic writing or arithmetic skills. More students can compete for advanced learning opportunities and seek to solve grand problems. More students can celebrate the joy of lifelong learning.

Questions for Reflection and Discussion

1. Reflect on your educational experiences. Where was a mastery approach used and where was an exposure model used? What were the outcomes for you?
2. Consider a topic which you presently, or may in the future, teach. How might you teach this topic to ensure mastery? What popular exposure methods might you have to guard against relying on?
3. If we have in fact set up an educational model that inhibits overachievement, what societal implications might ensue?

USING TECHNOLOGY

KEY TAKEAWAY

Technology is a major part of your students' lives. It is how they experience their world. New technologies need to be evaluated using the simple question "Is this tool an aid or an impediment to learning?" If it is an aid, learn it and use it.

The role of technology in the classroom is a complex and ever changing one. Whether you believe it has a primary or secondary place in the classroom, the trend towards its increasing use is crystal clear. More teachers use more technology in their classrooms every year. Administrators devote increasing percentages of their budgets to its acquisition, maintenance, upgrading, and usage. Technology committees have arisen in most school districts and universities to help guide, and some would say encourage, the use of technology in the classroom. And teachers are being hired and evaluated based on their technological proficiency. There is no doubt that the technology age in the classroom has arrived.

And this demand is not going to abate soon, if ever. Your young students are growing up in a very different world than you experienced. Technology is much more a part of their everyday existence. iPods and iPads, Google and Android, phones that provide instant answers, and of course the life lines of Facebook and Twitter dominate life. These are their staples of life; these are your students' reference points. It is important to remember that this is all they have known. They do not see these as incredible inventions or development; they are simply the tools of life.

These young students will soon be, and in some cases already are, the teachers of today and tomorrow. As this process unfolds over the next ten years there will be fewer discussions of technology in the classroom as if it is something new to integrate. It will simply be a part of educational life in the same way that it is part of life itself—seamlessly interwoven into daily existence.

The train of technology is not returning to the station. Technology will only be replaced by newer technology. These are the realities, whether we celebrate them or not. The underlying issues though will always remain the same, regardless of the specific piece of technology being examined: What is its role in the learning process?

Therefore, it would not make sense in a book like this to review specific technology tools and their educational usefulness. By the time of publication new instruments and tools will have overtaken the ones we are discussing today. It thus makes more sense for us to consider the issue of technology more generally, on a more macroscopic level. If we can propose a way of thinking about technology in the classroom that goes beyond any one time period's specific technology, teachers of today and tomorrow will benefit equally.

This rather ambitious undertaking may in fact be more easily accomplished than it might at first seem. If we continue to remember that learning is the goal in every classroom, our analysis can be focused in this realm. More specifically, a rather simple question might summarize this analytic approach best: Are our new tools an aid or an impediment to learning? If we can answer this question clearly, it will be easy to draw conclusions regarding technology's role in the classroom. And if we conclude that any piece of technology might aid our students' learning, we then can begin to examine how an excellent teacher might use this technology to help students learn in her classroom.

This approach of course somewhat begs the question as to how we might measure whether new technologies are aiding or impeding learning. No doubt there are well designed research projects collecting relevant assessment data in this realm right now. But we cannot simply wait for those answers. Data collection and the process of science are slow, and technological developments are here now. Thus, at this juncture since much of that data is not yet available to us, our analysis must be more logical and qualitative than quantitative.

Logical analysis suggests that you should use technology if it allows for or encourages one of the following four learning experiences. First, you know that students in your classroom come to you with very different learning styles. Some are more visual while others are strong auditory processors. Some learn best experientially, and others seem to understand when there is some kinesthetic involvement. Each of us has a learning styles profile that highlights our learning style strengths and weaknesses. New classroom technologies often allow you to present lessons using multiple learning modalities, rather than the one or two you have often been limited to in the past. When technology allows you to reach all of the learners in the classroom, rather than just the subset of learners who may process the world in the same way in which you feel comfortable teaching, technology has almost certainly been a benefit to learning.

Technology can help you to remove the geographic and economic limitations of your classrooms. It can help expose your students to people and places which would remain inaccessible to them. Many of your students will not have the opportunity to travel the world, let alone explore the frontiers beyond our planet. Technology can take them there. Your students may never have the opportunity to hear the voices of people from different cultures, the ideas of people who think very differently, or the sound of foreign languages. Technology can offer these experiences to your students. Again, technology used in this way is a benefit.

When used correctly, technology can help your students learn more effectively and efficiently. We know that students remember material best when they process it deeply. A series of memory experiments over the past 40 years has demonstrated that we remember best when we process deeply and meaningfully, and when the mode of presentation matches well with the mode of retrieval. The most famous of these studies occurred back in the 1970's. Craik and Lockhart (1972) proposed the "Levels of Processing" model of memory. They demonstrated that people remembered best when they used something called Type II processing rather than Type I processing. Type II processing involves strategies that encourage "deep" or meaningful processing, rather than shallow processing. Strategies that help us to make meaning out of information, that allow us to apply our knowledge, or that force us to relate it to other already known material are all examples of deep processing. When technology can help you teach in a way that allows, encourages, or even forces your students to process the material in more meaningful ways, you have a greater chance that they will remember the material better. When concepts are not simply memorized, but when students can see their importance, examine how they can be applied in different scenarios, and connect them to other concepts, learning is likely to improve. When our technology helps us to do this, it will be an aid to learning.

Finally, technology can help you increase student involvement in your classroom, and in so doing energizing and empowering your students to learn. Most of us believe at least intuitively that we learn best when we are emotionally engaged with the material. We learn best when we are active processors of the material. We learn best when our passions are stirred. Technology can help you here as well.

Allow me to use one simple example from today's technology. Many teachers are implementing "clickers" into their classrooms. These are simple devices that allow students to vote, answer questions, and register task completion all with a simple remote control hand held device. Using these clickers, everyone participates, and when they don't, you as the teacher are immediately aware. Gone are the days when only one student wanted to raise his hand to answer questions. Clickers engage students and force their active participation. Everyone is engaged and involved, and this is no doubt a good thing.

The same type of analysis can help guide us away from technologies which might interfere with learning. Some forms of technology seem to force students to use one style of processing, rather than opening them up to multiple styles. This is problematic for every student who does not naturally process in this way. Just as the old style lecture classroom in college was wonderful only for the auditory processor, some of our new technologies can be equally limiting. Technologies that force visual processing on those who process better auditorially, or vice versa, need to be avoided or at least implemented into an organized plan that offers students multiple processing options.

We all know that we learn best when we focus our attention. Divided attention is not conducive to encoding and learning (Craik, Govani, Naveh-Benjamin, and Anderson, 1996). Distractions impede learning. This is important to remember when evaluating technology in the classroom. You can help your students significantly if you ask yourself whether the technologies being employed still allow your students to focus, rather than divide, their attention.

Finally, some technologies can actually encourage more passive processing than active processing. This cannot be good for learning. You want your students to be active thinkers, to engage with the material, to question and wonder, and to process deeply. Technologies that encourage passivity work against you in these goals, and thus should be avoided.

In essence the ideal role of technology is simple. Asking yourself whether any specific piece or combination of pieces of technology aids or interferes with learning should guide your decision making, no matter what amazing inventions are around the corner.

Questions for Reflection and Discussion

1. Consider a newer piece of technology. How might it impact learning in the classroom? Will it aid or impede learning? Why?
2. Why do you think we always rush to implement the latest technology in our classrooms, well before we have carefully assessed its role in learning?
3. Why do you think we sometimes resist new technologies in our classrooms, often before we have truly evaluated whether they might aid or impede learning?

ASSESSING LEARNING

KEY TAKEAWAY

Assessing how well and what students have learned has become essential in justifying educational approaches and expenses. Assessment of learning can be made more valid and meaningful by following ten guidelines that will help you discharge your duty to fairly and meaningfully document your students' progress.

Assessment of learning is an increasingly important but complex issue. As a teacher you will be required to demonstrate that your students are learning and that you are doing a competent job. More importantly, you will want to know this information for planning reasons. You will want to know how well your students are learning with the techniques you are using. This knowledge of course will become the foundation for all of your future educational planning, from setting goals to trying new strategies. Quite simply, the results of these assessments will guide your future teaching.

In light of this I am encouraging you to examine how you will assess learning in your classroom. It is right and just that you do this, but it is also practical. You will be increasingly asked to justify your methods and outcomes, a trend which is not likely to change any time soon. Thus I offer the following ten guidelines designed to help you undertake this complex and important process.

Guideline 1: Set and Communicate Clear Goals

Setting the table for assessment starts with goal setting. You should have clearly established learning goals and priorities in your classroom and courses. If you teach in a K-12 public school, these goals are likely set for you, probably both at the state level and at the school district level. If you teach at a higher level, you will have more discretion over the setting of these goals.

You should ask yourself these three questions about these learning goals:

- Are they complete?
- Are they specific enough to allow for fair measurement?
- Are they achievable?

These goals will form the foundation for all of your assessments. As such, you must clearly communicate these to your students. It can be quite helpful to revisit them before and after every assessment activity. That is, you should explain how each assessment is related to your learning goals, and this should be discussed when you give the assignment and when you return the graded assignment.

Guideline 2: Assess Relevant "Knowledge"

Ask yourself what kinds of "knowledge" you emphasize and want your students to carry away from your class. Is it factual knowledge? Is it procedural knowledge? Is it a set of specific skills? Is it the application of concepts? Is it the integration of theory? Whatever types of "knowledge" you have deemed important and emphasize in class, these should be the foci of your goals and your assessments.

Guideline 3: Teach Through Assessments

It is important to remember that assessment of learning can be a learning experience in itself. Assessment activities that ask students to apply concepts, to analyze ideas, or to integrate knowledge do double duty. They allow you to assess for learning but they also give students the opportunity to deepen their understanding while being assessed. This is a double win.

Therefore, exams should be just part of the learning assessment process. You want students to show you what they have learned. Exams are limiting in this way. Be sure to build in projects, papers, and application exercises that allow students to demonstrate learning outside of traditional exams. After all, in the real world students will have to apply their knowledge, not just remember it.

Guideline 4: Construct Fair Exams

Much of your assessment of learning is likely to focus on exams. In light of this, some detailed suggestions are in order.

Before you construct an exam, rank order the five to seven most important concepts covered since the last exam. Start your test construction process by creating numerous questions designed to thoroughly assess student knowledge in each of these five to seven key areas. Only after this is complete should you consider constructing questions on topics of secondary importance. You should almost never construct questions on topics of tertiary importance.

Your exam should allow students to demonstrate what they have learned. They should not be exercises in demonstrating what they have not learned. A good test uses different types of questions throughout. Multiple choice questions allow for recognition, but are limited in their ability to allow students to demonstrate what they have learned. Short-essay, identifies, and long-essays give the student the opportunity to demonstrate what they have learned.

With each exam question that you construct, you should ask yourself the following series of questions:

- Does this question tap into one of the knowledge areas I think is most important for this class?
- Does this question assess learning of a key (not trivial) component of the class material?
- Is this question phrased in a clear and straightforward manner so that I can be sure that I am assessing knowledge of the desired concept rather than decoding of complex questions?

If the answer to any of these questions is "no", the question should not be on the exam.

This suggests an interesting exercise for even seasoned instructors. Take an old exam and go through each question. Next to each question write the letter H, M, or L. Write an "H" if you believe the information or task addressed in that question is of high importance to the course. Write an "M" if you believe the information or task is of medium importance, and an "L" if it is of low importance. Tally your percentage of H, M, and L's. Is your percentage of "L's" very low? If not, perhaps that exam needs revision.

This of course leads to the issue of using prepackaged or "book" tests. While convenient and thorough, there are common problems with book tests. First, the test author does not know what you emphasized as the important learning material in class. Therefore, many questions will correspond to topics you did not consider important enough to raise in class. If it was not important enough to raise in class, it is hard to see how it would be important enough to examine. Second, book tests do not use your language and word choice. Students will have heard you explain concepts using your own unique words and examples. Book tests will use a different vocabulary. Moreover, because book tests are often not written by the author of the textbook, the word choice on the tests will not even reflect the language of the textbook. This creates a significant problem in assessment. You want your assessment to be a valid measure of the mastery of concepts taught in class. You do not want it to be a measure of vocabulary or reading comprehension. Thus, if you must use book tests, it is wise to at least edit them for word choice and topics so that the questions correspond more closely to what was covered in class.

Guideline 5: Make Sure Your Assessment Is Valid

Validity is a concept that is often written about in psychological and educational literature. At its most basic level, a valid test is simply one which measures what it purports to measure. A chemistry test that asks students to balance equations has clear "face validity." It appears to measure exactly what it is supposed to measure. A history test that integrates interpretation of a poem, however, might have questionable validity. Make sure your assessments appear to measure what they are supposed to measure.

Guideline 6: Guide Your Students

Students should have a very clear idea of what to study. Your goal is student learning. If you think something is important enough for them to learn, then you should tell them that explicitly. Whether this means that they should get a formal study sheet/ guide or not may be somewhat dependent upon the course material and level of course, but in general it means exactly that.

Guideline 7: Set Clear Criteria for Assignment Grading

With each assigned paper and project, you must be clear on how you will assess it. Grading of exams, papers, and projects must pass muster. Being clear ahead of time as to how you will assess performance is essential. Just as employees want to know what standards will be used by employers to assess job performance, so too do students desire this in the classroom. The best way to handle this is to use grading rubrics for non-objective assignments. Papers, projects, and interviews should be graded using a grading rubric which was shared with students before they completed the assignment. This lends a bit of objectivity and fairness to what many see as a very subjective exercise.

Guideline 8: Be Clear about Term Grades

End of term grading is the necessary outcome of class assessment. It too must be addressed in your communication to students, whether that be in formal syllabi or less formal means with younger students. Students should have a very clear understanding of how each assessment activity will contribute to their grade, how much each assessment activity is worth in points or percentages, and thus how their final grade will be calculated. Points or percentage ranges should then be tied to specific letter grades which will be used when reporting grades.

Guideline 9: Don't Fall for the Trap of Apriori Grade Distribution

Grade distribution is an area of much unneeded consternation, particularly amongst less experienced faculty. While some schools and departments require that grade distributions correspond to specific frequency distributions (e.g. grades should be normally distributed), this is in practice rather uncommon. In fact, it makes more logical sense not to force-fit grades to apriori distributions. If all students in the class have achieved your learning goals to at least a satisfactory level, then it is illogical to assign any grade lower than C. If all students have excelled or failed to learn, your distribution will be quite skewed. Of course, if many students have in fact failed, the course most likely has a more serious problem than an assessment issue.

Guideline 10: Empower Students

If you are feeling particularly adventuresome, you might use the assessment process to empower students to begin to take more control over their performance. Giving students choices is an excellent way to do this. Obviously, this guideline will depend heavily on what grade level you are teaching. Most young students will not be developmentally prepared for this level of responsibility. Older students, however, might be.

At the most basic level, such empowerment might include giving students choices as to which essay to answer on an exam. This is a common and good practice. However, you can go further than this. Students might be given the option of writing a final paper or taking a final exam. In a more senior level class, students could even be given more control over the make-up of their final grade. If the instructor indicated at the start of the course that all students would have to complete three exams, one project, and one paper, the instructor could also allow the student input as to the relative weighting of each assignment. Before, or immediately after the first exam, students could be asked whether they wanted all five assignments equally weighted, exams weighted more than the paper/projects, or paper/projects weighted more than the exams. Handing this decision, within reason, over to the student empowers them to take more control over their learning and to develop an understanding of their own learning and performance styles, an important metacognitive achievement.

Conducting reliable and valid assessments is your duty as an educator. You will be asked to defend your assessment measures and document your results. Following these guidelines should be a significant first step in that process.

Questions for Reflection and Discussion

1. Has assessment of learning assumed too much or too little attention in recent years in the field of education? Why do you think discussions of assessment of learning have become so popular in our society?
2. How will you be sure that the forms of assessment you choose are both fair and valid?
3. Which of the ten guidelines will present the biggest challenge for you? Why do you think that is?

PART VI

IMPROVING YOUR CRAFT

In this section you will be encouraged to become a true professional by seeking feedback on your work and studying those who have mastered your profession.

STUDYING SUCCESSFUL TEACHERS

KEY TAKEAWAY

Take time to purposefully learn from teachers who are already masters. Observe them and talk to them, always staying open to their feedback.

During your "apprenticeship" you studied the teachers who taught you. While this was a great opportunity to observe and learn, this was almost accidental learning. It is unlikely that back then you had a clear sense that education and teaching were your life goals. Moreover, your perspective then was as a student, often a very young student. While this gave you a valuable and unique perspective, your main goal in that classroom was not to learn how to teach, but rather simply to learn.

Now it is time to more purposefully learn from the experts. This learning can be done through a combination of observation and inquiry. By visiting the classrooms of master teachers, and then talking with them about their craft, you now have the opportunity to more intentionally observe and learn teaching excellence.

Step one in this process involves simply visiting the classrooms of master teachers. If your desire is to teach grade school, start there. If you want to be a college professor, begin there. Do not worry about asking to visit other teachers' classrooms. Most excellent teachers will welcome you into their classrooms. Their confidence in their skills will be obvious the minute you request a visit.

Be an active observer and do not expect to observe everything in just one visit. Plan for multiple visits. Some of the major areas you want to directly observe include the structure of the lesson, how the teacher bridges and scaffolds from one topic to another, her interaction with the classroom as a whole and her interaction with individuals, her use of her own personality as a teaching tool, the integration of technology into the lesson, her communication tools and style, her manner of checking to make sure students are actually learning, and her general presence in the room. Take notes but observe carefully. Jot down questions you will want to address to her during step two of this process.

Be sure to ask for copies of important classroom materials before your visit as you will want to observe with a specific context in mind. If you are observing a grade school classroom, ask for a copy of the lesson plan. If you are observing a high school or college classroom, make sure you have reviewed the teacher's syllabus before observing.

It is often helpful to broaden step one beyond visiting classrooms of teachers at the level you wish to teach. That is, it can be helpful to observe master teachers at levels above and beneath the education level you have as your career goal. For a high school teacher, having a good sense of excellent teaching in both junior high school and college can be quite informative. Through observing master teachers at various levels you get a better sense of where your learners have come from and what you should be preparing them for.

These observations will help in your lesson planning when you are in charge of your own classroom. It will also be of significant help in trying to understand learning failures in your classroom. Almost inevitably some students will lack certain foundational skills necessary to make them successful in your classroom. Having observed master teachers who taught younger students these foundational skills will help you to design curricula and lessons that can help remedy their current deficits. Knowing where your students are headed will also help in your lesson planning. Knowing what master teachers, who are toiling at the next level, need for their students to succeed at this higher level can help you prepare them now.

Step two of your study of successful teachers involves interviewing the teachers you have observed. The observation is not enough. You must now go beyond this to truly understand the motivations, strategies, and skills of the master teacher. A thirty minute interview or conversation should get you that crucial data. Again, the experienced excellent teacher will give you this time. These teachers understand that part of their mission is to help the next generation of educators.

While this interview can be quite informal, you will want to have questions prepared ahead of time. I offer you the following list of ten guide questions to start this process. This is certainly not to say that these ten questions are mandatory or even best for your interview. Rather, these ten questions are offered as a starting point and as a stimulus for you to develop questions uniquely tailored to your learning needs as well as the expertise of the teacher you observed. With this in mind then, these ten questions should be considered:

1. How do you get students excited about learning?
2. What is the best advice you ever got about teaching (and perhaps the worst as well)?
3. How do you go about forming a learning community in your classroom?
4. What is the best thing you do as a teacher?
5. What blocks people from becoming good teachers?
6. If you were mentoring a new teacher, what specific advice would you give?
7. Why do you think some teachers seem to burn out and can it be prevented?
8. In your experience, how long does it take to become a good teacher?
9. What do you do to make sure you stay current in the field?
10. What do you do to make sure you continue to be an excellent teacher?

These are merely guide questions. Remember you will be talking with an expert. The last thing you want to do is over-structure the interview. An overly structured interview deprives the interviewee of going beyond the limits of your questions. It would be too arrogant of us to think that our questions will really capture what each master teacher has to share. So build in room for the teacher to go "off script" and share her wisdom with you.

So much can be learned about teaching by simply watching and talking with master teachers. Fortunately for us these skilled individuals are also often quite generous with their time. Just try to remember years from now to pay back the favor when you are the master teacher and a newbie contacts you for the same type of interview.

Questions for Reflection and Discussion

1. Review the list of suggested interview questions above. Add five questions of your own. Reflect on why you have added those five questions. What is it about these five questions that you think will help your own teaching?
2. Do you think one ever sees themselves as having achieved the level of "master teacher"?
3. What things do you fear might prevent you from becoming a master teacher?

STAYING CURRENT

KEY TAKEAWAY

Stay up-to-date in the field of education, in your discipline, and in the world of your students. Let your students reverse roles here and teach you about their world. Stay open to new ideas and new experiences.

It's hard to stay current. Keeping up to date in our rapidly changing world can feel overwhelming. In fact, the older you get, the harder it is. Yet, it is very important if you desire a lengthy successful career rather than a quick positive first impression.

As a teacher it is important to stay current in three spheres. First, you must stay up to date in the field of education. New terms and technologies flood the field every year. It is important that you become fluent in this ever-changing language. You must always be aware of what other educators are trying, whether or not their attempts prove successful or not. You must be able to converse with your colleagues about these new ideas. Sometimes these conversations will allow you to become informed, while at other times you will be doing the informing. In either case, you will be left out of these conversations if your educational knowledge is not current. And make no mistake about it, you do not want to be left out of these conversations. If you are left out, you cannot impact the process. You cannot be a strong spokesperson for what you believe is good education. You cannot be a mentor to the new generation of educators.

Second, you must stay current in your field, in your specific discipline. There is little worse than a teacher who is teaching old or even disproven theories, outdated ideas, or incorrect information. Almost every field changes over time, some much more than others. If you teach science or technology, change will hit you harder. A much greater proportion of your time will be spent keeping up. If you teach history, change in your discipline will still affect you. While it may be true that most of the facts of history will not change, this is not completely true. New historical discoveries are made every day, some mundane and some profound. Just yesterday's news is new history for today. And new historical theories, analyses, and research techniques are proposed frequently. So, although the pace of change may be more accelerated in some disciplines than others, change impacts all disciplines. It is your responsibility to stay current.

Third, you must stay current with the world of your students. Our society is changing rapidly. New technologies and ways of communication are altering the way we live. Your students will not know the old ways. They will only know the new ways. The "new" ways will be the only way for them. While it is okay to reminisce about the old days and old ways, they are never coming back. You must embrace these changes, particularly in the technological world, if you expect to connect with your students.

Your knowledge of their world though must go beyond being familiar with the newer technologies. You must be aware of their "world." What do they watch on television? What music do they listen to? What are their relationship expectations? What careers capture their fancy? What do they talk about? Meet your students where they are at. Use examples from their world, not yours. Make assignments relevant to their lives. Understand how whatever you are teaching relates to who and where they are today. This is an essential educational connection that good teachers make. You can succeed in making that connection only if you stay current.

The process of staying current allows for an additional opportunity, a secondary benefit. You will need help in the process of staying current. You will need to be taught. This is a wonderful opportunity to connect with your students in a very different way. Allowing them to be your teacher, to explain new ideas, technologies, and mores to you can be a powerful role reversal. In this simple action you communicate so much to them. You model lifelong learning for them. You show them that no one knows everything and that everyone needs to be open to learning. You demonstrate to them how to be a good student, an active and inquisitive learner, an open minded individual. This lesson may be a far more important life lesson than the specific content that you are teaching. Allowing them to teach and lead you can be a powerful educational experience for you both.

Staying current does not mean being untrue to who you are, to your own history. You do not need to pretend to be younger than you are. You do not need to speak or dress differently than you do. You must be comfortable in your own identity and staying current should not challenge that. Rather staying current involves staying open, open to the process of learning.

Staying current need not be hard work, but it will be work. Much can be accomplished here with a simple attitudinal approach of always being open to new ideas and new experiences. This comes naturally for many educators and this is a fortunate thing. But sometimes it will challenge you. New ways can be hard to understand, let alone accept. We tend to cling to our comfortable ways of understanding the world and of doing things. Being a good educator will almost certainly push you out of that comfort zone. Really working hard at least to cognitively understand the new ways will go a long way with your students, even if you conclude in the end that these new ways are not for you.

Questions for Reflection and Discussion

1. Project out another ten or twenty years. What "comfortable ways" of yours might be challenged by subsequent generations? How can you be sure you will respond in an open manner?
2. Think back about some of the many teachers you have had. Can you think of one or two who clearly communicated this desire to stay current? How did they communicate that to you? Were they able to stay true to themselves in the process?
3. In contrast, can you think of any teachers who did not communicate the desire to stay current? How did they communicate that? What impact do you think it had on their teaching and on your learning?

WELCOMING FEEDBACK I: STAKEHOLDERS

KEY TAKEAWAY
You cannot improve if you do not allow yourself to get honest feedback. This feedback can come from various stakeholders. Stakeholders can include students, parents, peers, and supervisors.

One of the best ways to learn, or improve, your craft as a teacher is to use valuable feedback from others. In order for this feedback to be useful and helpful, however, a well-planned approach to seeking and receiving the feedback is important.

Education today likes to use the word "stakeholders." Stakeholders are those people who have a "stake" in your work, who will benefit or suffer from your success or failure. They are groups who are invested in your success. The stakeholders in your teaching are many, and feedback can be secured from each of these groups. In fact, each group has valuable and important, but very different, information to offer. Four groups of stakeholders can provide you with very valuable feedback on your performance as a teacher.

The first group includes the most direct stakeholders—your students. Depending upon their age and developmental level, they may be able to offer you very direct feedback on your teaching performance. These are the only stakeholders who see your work every day and who benefit or fail based directly on your performance. In this way, they are the most important group of stakeholders.

Seeking and welcoming feedback from this group is essential to bettering your teaching. Students can uniquely comment on such issues as how well you show respect for them, how well you understand individual differences, how reasonable your expectations are, how fair you are in evaluation and assessment, how well prepared and organized you are, how tolerant you are, how clear your goals are, and how well they have learned in your classroom. While seeking such data from very young students who may not be able to engage in this reflective exercise is not likely to be productive, students older than elementary school should be able to handle this task. Such direct feedback from your students is the most valuable feedback you can receive.

A second group of stakeholders are the parents of your students. This group does not have direct access to your performance as a teacher, but rather sees and experiences its effects quite directly. This group has different feedback to offer than your students themselves. In fact, when students are quite young, this feedback often must replace direct student feedback. Even when students are older or more mature and you can receive direct feedback from them, parents have much to offer.

Parents can give you feedback on aspects of your performance your students do not directly encounter. Parents will certainly be able to tell you how well you communicate with them. Is your communication consistent, clear, timely, and helpful? Such communication is often essential in helping students address learning struggles well before they have failed and in time for effective intervention. Parents can also give you feedback on how you are perceived by your students outside of the classroom. Are you perceived as willing to be helpful? Are you perceived as empowering? Do students respect you? Do you excite learning in students? These are important pieces of information you may not be able to get elsewhere.

Finally, parents can also comment on how effective you have been in teaching their children. How successful have you been in helping students use the knowledge and skills they are learning? They will often know quite clearly what their child has learned in your classroom. Perhaps more importantly, they will be able to comment on how well that knowledge has been retained and applied outside the classroom. We all hope that we are educating for life, not for the four walls of the classroom.

Colleagues can offer you a unique evaluation of your work as well. Colleagues or peers are the ones who know the real struggles of your everyday work. They do not have unrealistic expectations, nor do they tend to condone underperformance. They understand the limitations of the educational setting but balance it with the understanding that a colleague's poor performance makes their own jobs more difficult. Your colleagues are often the ones who can give you the most concrete feedback and suggestions. While it is always somewhat anxiety provoking to invite others into your classroom, the value of such feedback is worth the risk. Their value lies less in an evaluation of how well your students are learning and more in suggestions for improving your work.

Three key questions should guide such a peer review. First, your colleague should be asked to suggest any concrete changes you might implement to become a better teacher. Such a specific question avoids the trap of asking them to simply evaluate your performance, a vague question which usually results in generic evaluative statements. It allows your colleague to offer ideas without having to be directly critical of you, someone whom they probably like as a person or enjoy interacting with in the teachers' lounge or at the mailboxes.

Second, you should ask your colleague whether there are any specific educational activities which they use which might fit your teaching style, students, and classroom. Here a colleague has the opportunity to talk about something that has been successful for them, something we all like to do. If this idea might improve your students' education, wonderful.

Finally, a more daring question can be posed. "Did you see anything in my teaching that you would like to incorporate in yours?" This is a better question than asking "What did I do well?" This latter question is too easy to finesse, to avoid, to answer with platitudes. The more daring question is challenging, and the delay in answering, or the content of the response, can often be quite telling.

The fourth and final group of stakeholders is your supervisors. Chairpersons, principals, and deans can provide you with a very different type of feedback than other groups. Sometimes these individuals have significant educational experience. Sometimes they are your wise elders who have successfully managed the same classrooms you are now struggling to handle. Sometimes these are veteran teachers who have "seen it all." When this is the case, their feedback on your teaching is quite valuable. Such feedback, when offered with concrete suggestions rather than only evaluative statements, can lead you to real improvement quickly.

Even when these administrators are not veteran teachers, they can offer valuable feedback of a different kind. They bring to the table a different perspective, different goals, and different demands. Their more macro perspective likely focuses more on how your work fits into the larger educational system of the school. This contrasts with the more micro level analysis of your teaching offered by your colleagues. How does your work fit into the school's and the community's goals for its young citizens? How does your work reflect and support the mission of the entire academic institution? How can you improve your work to support your colleagues as you work together to accomplish grand educational goals? This more macro level feedback can be uniquely handled by big-picture thinking administrators.

The stakeholders in the education of your students have much to offer in helping you become a better teacher, in the classroom and beyond. Each group has unique perspectives. You must take the risk of asking for each group's feedback if you have the hope of mastering, or at least improving at, your craft.

Questions for Reflection and Discussion

1. Are there other stakeholders not identified in these four groups who might also offer important feedback to you? What types of unique feedback might they offer?
2. Which stakeholding group will be most difficult for you to seek feedback from? Why?
3. Knowing yourself, how might you best prepare yourself to seek feedback from each group?

WELCOMING FEEDBACK II:
MANAGING THE PROCESS

KEY TAKEAWAY

Work actively to receive feedback in a way that will be helpful to your professional growth. Both qualitative and quantitative feedback can be helpful. Staying non-defensive is essential to profiting from the feedback.

Teaching is a very personal endeavor. Receiving feedback on anything so intimate can be scary. In order for this feedback to be productive and helpful, then, you must manage the process actively.

As we discussed in the last essay, feedback can come from several different groups of stakeholders: students themselves, parents, colleagues, and supervisors. While the content of this feedback will likely differ, so should the format. For some groups, quantitative feedback is in order. Almost always, substantive commentary is helpful as well.

When asking students and parents for feedback, quantitative data is very important. Quantitative data allows you to get specific feedback on certain predefined questions. That is, they guide the evaluator towards the areas you feel are most important. Moreover, it insures that you receive that feedback in a way that you can readily digest it. Quantitative feedback allows you to notice trends, to identify shortcomings and strengths that are robust, and to minimize the skewing of results that can occur when one individual or small group feels very strongly about your work, whether those feelings are strongly positive or negative.

Allowing students and parents an opportunity for substantive commentary can be a helpful complement to the quantitative data. Here stakeholders can address strong feelings, offer unique feedback, and comment on areas you might not have seen as of primary importance. Such open ended questions give stakeholders a chance to offer specific praises and criticisms.

When asking for feedback from colleagues and supervisors, it is this substantive, or qualitative commentary that usually offers the most helpful feedback. While it may be that you are required to receive a quantitative assessment from these groups as well, perhaps as part of a job performance evaluation or promotion process, such quantitative evaluations here are often quite limiting. Remember, the types of information you want here are critiques and suggestions from colleagues who face the same demands and who are successful. Here you want ideas that work. You want to be told where your shortcomings are and how you can quickly redress them. You want specific ideas for improvement.

In seeking evaluations from colleagues and supervisors, you want to make sure that you are not restricting their observations in any way. Offering feedback simply on the basis of one class visit is often not particularly useful. Multiple visits are better. In addition, restricting comments and suggestions to areas directly observed is also limiting. Asking colleagues to review your course materials like lesson plans, syllabi, exams, handouts, and homework assignments will result in a far more comprehensive and likely more valid assessment. Moreover, it will prompt much richer feedback and more detailed suggestions.

An additional part of managing this process is preparing yourself emotionally to receive feedback. As you know, teaching is a very intimate yet public process. You are on display, and your effectiveness can be easily evaluated. This creates strong feelings of vulnerability which must be managed. Managing this part of the process involves giving careful consideration to which particular stakeholders to ask for input and preparing yourself to receive the results.

It is generally accepted that you ask all students or parents to participate in this process. It would not make sense to exclude anyone and then believe that the results were in any way representative. However, this does not prevent you from requesting additional information from subsets of these larger groups. Perhaps there is a group of students or parents whose opinions you especially value. Asking them for additional feedback can be helpful, as long as such a self-selected group is not simply one you believe will tell you what you want to hear. As long as this group is chosen for their ability to provide rich feedback, these additions can complement your overall results.

While you usually do not have any choice over your supervisors, picking the right colleagues so that your peer review is productive is very important. There are a few basic issues which you might consider in this process. First, choosing colleagues who have achieved at least as much, if not more, than you is generally a good idea. If a colleague has already been successful at your level, they will likely have much to offer. Asking a colleague who has less experience and success is not very logical. At the university level this means asking for reviews from those who have achieved higher ranks, like associate or full professor, rather than those at lower ranks, such as instructors or assistant professors, is a good plan. At elementary, middle, and high school levels, asking colleagues with tenure or more teaching experience can accomplish the same goal.

Moreover, you want to ask colleagues who will be able to provide you with balanced, fair, detailed, and helpful evaluations and suggestions. Asking colleagues who are insecure, perpetually negative, or unable to appreciate individual differences in teaching is not usually helpful. Asking peers who are tolerant, fair, observant, encouraging, and positively challenging is a far better plan.

Receiving feedback is understandably an anxiety provoking situation. Emotionally preparing yourself to receive feedback is incredibly important to making this a productive process. You must be in a place where you can hear, process, fairly evaluate, and act on the feedback if this process is to be productive. Being overly anxious blocks your listening and your learning. Being defensive changes the conversation. Lashing out punishes the invited messenger and lessens the likelihood for honest feedback and future participation.

In order to emotionally prepare yourself, you should structure the feedback experience. You should not examine quantitative data until you are settled, calm, and ready. You should not talk to your evaluators when you are pressed for time, stressed about other issues, or not in a quiet and private space. Discussing feedback immediately after a class, in the front of the classroom, or in the hallway between classes is usually a disastrous idea. Such exchanges by their very nature are usually shallow and perfunctory. Moreover, such quick exchanges can result in simple misunderstandings and miscommunications. It is doubtful that you asked for feedback in order to receive such unhelpful input.

Receiving written feedback from colleagues and supervisors must be planned as well. Do not ask for, or provide, quick e-mail messages. These fail in the same way that hallway conversations fail. Word choice can be careless and lead to misinterpretation. Style can mistakenly communicate unintended messages. Rather, when written feedback is part of the process, asking for a considered and detailed write up that addresses the issues you have requested, like ideas for improvement, is a much better plan. Moreover, following up receipt of such written feedback with a face to face meeting can prevent damaging misunderstandings and misinterpretations.

Receiving the feedback is not the end of the process. Deciding what to do with the feedback is a necessary last step. This should again be a carefully considered step. Willy-nilly implementation of suggestions is not likely to improve your teaching. Rather, carefully evaluating each idea, examining whether or not you agree with the analysis, and translating it into a plan or method that fits your style should all be steps that occur before actual implementation.

You may strongly disagree with one of the observations or suggestions. Strong reactions should be carefully considered. Perhaps you are correct and the observer has misunderstood. Perhaps this is an area around which you are defensive and have difficulty hearing feedback? At other times you may agree with an observation but disagree with a plan to address the deficiency. Developing a better plan which suits your style is a productive result of such a disagreement. Discarding the entire idea is not.

It is highly unlikely that you can improve as an educator without welcoming feedback, but you must remember how vulnerable this process makes you. Choosing the appropriate type of data, selecting those who can provide valuable feedback, and preparing yourself emotionally for the feedback process can make for a powerful learning experience for any educator.

Questions for Reflection and Discussion

1. Knowing yourself, your personality, your emotions, and your sensitivities, how hard will the feedback process be for you? What aspect of the process might make you feel most vulnerable? Knowing this, how will you best prepare yourself for this process?
2. What types of people is it difficult for you to receive feedback from? What specific characteristics of others tend to block the communicative process for you? How will that impact your choice of colleagues in the feedback process?
3. Put together a plan for yourself as to how you might structure the feedback process so that it will be beneficial for you? What types of evaluative information will you seek out? From whom? What process will you put in place so that you will be able to translate the feedback into a personal improvement plan?

PART VII

CONCLUSIONS

You are on your journey now. Enjoy the process.

CHAPTER 25

FOLLOWING THE GOLDEN RULE (OF TEACHING)

<table>
<tr><td>KEY TAKEAWAY</td></tr>
<tr><td>Treat each student as you would want your son or daughter treated.</td></tr>
</table>

Often it is helpful to reduce complex entities to their essences. In doing so, much of the complexity is stripped away and clarity ensues. Certainly, learning to become an excellent teacher is a long and complex process. However, at its core, perhaps one rule can guide you.

We have all heard of the "golden rule", usually stated as "treat others the way you would want to be treated." And truth be told, this is generally a sound rule for life. In teaching though, allow me to offer a very slight corollary to this rule as a way of guiding your interactions and decision making with students. Treat all of your students as you would want your own children treated in the classroom.

Rather than putting yourself in your student's shoes, imagine if it were your son or daughter as the student. How would you want him treated? How would you want teachers to interact with her? What teaching techniques would you want his teachers to use? What life lessons would you want her learning in the classroom? How would you want his learning assessed? How much would you like her teacher to know about her learning style or her disability? What characteristics would you want his teachers to have? What commitment to learning would you want her teachers to model? What commitment to improvement would you want his teachers to endorse?

Granted, situations will not always be this simple. Sometimes intense and complex problems will develop in your classroom and you will be at a loss as to how to act or work toward resolution. The golden rule of teaching, in this case, at least gives you a place to start. It will give you a quick reference point and a quick guide to action that you can re-examine later when time permits.

When time does permit, engage in the more complex analysis and deeper reflection that the particular challenge raises. By doing so, you will help to prepare yourself for similar issues and situations in the future. But you need time, and often consultation, to engage in this deeper work. Until that time, simply treat students the way you would want your own children treated.

CHAPTER 26

FINAL WORDS

KEY TAKEAWAY
Enjoy the journey!

You are well on your way now. Your journey is unfolding. It will be an exciting, invigorating, frustrating, maddening, hopeful, unpredictable, and often bittersweet one. You will meet students who fascinate you and those who frustrate you. You will empower many and fail to reach some. You will learn and develop along the way, always adding to your knowledge base, inviting new experiences and perspectives, and refining your craft until the day you leave the profession.

Many students will surprise you along the way. Allow that to happen. Don't jump to premature conclusions about how much a student can learn and grow. This is one of the most exciting things about teaching. Students who frustrated you, or whom you think you did not reach, might visit you years later to thank you for the life lessons. Remember, so much of what we teach lies dormant for years, only to be awakened by a new life event or experience. Don't demand immediate payoff for your lessons; some investments take years to show a profit.

You are a chapter in their book of life, but an incredibly important chapter in a book whose ending has not yet been written. You will help author that ending through your work, your connection, your passion, your zeal, your knowledge, your leadership, your instruction, and your mentoring.

As I wrote in the introduction, being a teacher is an incredible privilege. You are now on the way to using that privilege in the responsible way society should demand. Do not squander that opportunity. Few receive it. Rather, embrace it and it will embrace you back.

REFERENCES

Agathon, B. (1785). *The twelve virtues of a good teacher* (Gerald Rummery, trans 1998). Retrieved from www.napcis.org/12virtuesgoodteacher.pdf.

Americans with Disabilities Act of 1990, *Public Law* 101–336, 2, 104, Stat. 328 (1991).

Collins, Terry (n.d.). *Saint John Baptiste de La Salle: Frequently cited quotations.* Retrieved from www.delasalle.org.uk/resources/quotes.

Craik, F., Govani, R., Naveh-Benjamin, M., & Anderson, N. (1996). The effects of divided attention on encoding and retrieval processes in human memory. *Journal of Experimental Psychology: General, 125*(2), 159–180.

Craik, F. I. M., & Lockhart, R. S. (1972). Levels of processing: A framework for memory research. *Journal of Verbal Learning and Verbal Behavior, 11*, 671–684.

Csikszentmihalyi, M. (1990). *Flow: The psychology of optimal experience.* New York: Harper & Row Publishers, Inc.

FairTest (2007). *How standardized testing damages education.* Retrieved from http://www.fairtest.org.

Felder, R. M., & Soloman, B. A. (2012). *Index of learning styles.* Retrieved from http://www.ncscu.edu/felder-public/ILSpage.html.

Freedle, R. (2003). Correcting the SAT's ethnic and social-class bias: A method for reestimating SAT scores. *Harvard Educational Review, 73*(1), 1–43.

Garrett, M. T. (2010). Native Americans. In D. G. Hays & B. T. Erford (Eds.), *Developing multicultural counseling competence: A systems approach* (pp. 301–332). Upper Saddle River, NJ: Pearson Education, Inc.

Gladding, S. T. (2012). *Group work: A counseling specialty.* Upper Saddle River, NJ: Merrill Prentice Hall.

Greenwood, J. (1995). Personal Communication.

Hays, D. G., & McLeod, A. L. (2010). The culturally competent counselor. In D. G. Hays & B. T. Erford (Eds.), *Developing multicultural counseling competence: A systems approach* (pp. 1–31). Upper Saddle River, NJ: Pearson Education, Inc.

Heckman, J. J. (2010). *Interview with Professor James Heckman, noted scholar and Nobel Prize winner.* Retrieved from www. Unesco.org/new/en/worldconferenceonecc.

Heckman, J. J., Humphries, J. E., & Mader, N. S. (2010). The GED [Discussion paper No. 4975]. *The Institute for the Study of Labor.* Retrieved from http://ftp.iza.org/dp4975.pdf.

Helm, K. M., & James, L. (2010). Individuals and families of African descent. In D. G. Hays & B. T. Erford (Eds.), *Developing multicultural counseling competence: A systems approach* (pp. 193–215). Upper Saddle River, NJ: Pearson Education, Inc.

Hill, C., Corbett, C., & St. Rose, A. (2010). *Why so few? Women in science, technology, engineering, and mathematics.* Washington, DC: AAUW.

Hill, V. (2012). Personal Communication.

Individuals with Disabilities Educational Act, 20 U.S.C. 1401 (2004).

Jaschik, S. (2010, June 21). *New evidence of racial bias on SAT [Newspaper article].* Retrieved from http://www.insidehighered.com/news/2010/06/21/sat.

Lasallian Heritage: St. John Baptiste De La Salle (2012). Retrieved from www.lasalle2.org/english/heritage/history/hehijbdls.php.

Levine, M. (2002). *A mind at a time.* New York: Simon & Shuster.

Pashler, H., McDaniel, M., Rohrer, D., & Bjork, R. (2008). Learning styles: Concepts and evidence. *Psychological Science in the Public Interest 9*(3), 105–119.

Project Implicit (2011). Retrieved from https://implicit.harvard.edu/implicit/user/pimh/index.jsp.

Sadker, M., & Sadker, D. (1994). *Failing at fairness: How our schools cheat girls.* New York, NY: Touchstone.

REFERENCES

Santelices, M. V., & Wilson, M. (2010). Unfair treatment? The case of Freedle, the SAT, and the standardization approach to differential item functioning. *Harvard Educational Review, 80*(1), 106–133.

Surowiecki, J. (2005). *The wisdom of crowds.* United States of America: Anchor Books.

Tough, P. (2011, September). What if the secret to success is failure? *New York Times.* Retrieved from http://www.nytimes.com/2011/09/18/magazine/what-if-the-secret-to-success-is-failure.html? pagewanted=all.

INDEX